T0331000

# Technology-Based Teaching and Learning in Pakistani English Language Classrooms

Pakistan is the sixth most populous country in the world. Unexpectedly, the education system in Pakistan is quite orthodox in teaching and learning. There are numerous educational institutes in Pakistan but they are rigorously following conventions. There are problems with infrastructure, and in some areas, the basic facilities are also not there. Sometimes the classrooms are overpopulated, and sometimes there are places where no teacher is available to teach the students. There are instances where the basic infrastructure is not complete and there are no proper classrooms for teaching and learning. All these factors are causing a lot of problems for learners to compete in the modern world. English enjoys the status of official language in the country but, surprisingly, learning English is a troublesome area. There are problems not only in basic English language learning but also many second language learners face problems when they appear in international tests and competitive examinations. English language classrooms are usually boring and uninteresting. Therefore, this book is written with an aim to provide alternative solutions to the conventional methods by integrating modern technology tools in Pakistani classrooms. The scope of this book is widened for language researchers, policymakers, readers and administrators of the government to analyse some of the problems and issues mentioned in this book and develop a roadmap for better education.

Some of the key elements of this book are as follows:

- This is the first research-based book to explore some of the latest research tools in Pakistani classrooms.
- This book is based on research-based chapters.
- Shows pictures of local English language classrooms.
- Provides insights and practices for integrating modern methods in English language classrooms.

**Muhammad Mooneeb Ali** has a PhD in English Linguistics with more than 14 years of teaching experience in applied linguistics, English as a Second Language (ESL), English as a Foreign Language (EFL), Teaching of English as a

Foreign Language (TEFL), Teaching of English as a Second Language (TESL) and Teaching of English to the Students of Other Languages (TESOL). He has been an expert researcher with more than 50 research publications to his name. He has authored and compiled 40 academic books for graduate and postgraduate students. Working with the Higher Education Department, he has worked extensively with international organisations to promote English language learning. He is also the reviewer of many Web of Science and Scopus Indexed Journals.

# Advances in Digital Technologies for Smart Applications
*Series Editor: Saad Motahhir*

The *Advances in Digital Technologies for Smart Applications* series publishes leading-edge research on innovative digital technologies and their application in smart systems. Key topics include AI, IoT, blockchain, and their integration into various sectors, including finance, healthcare, and public governance.

*Data Analytics for Finance Using Python*
Nitin Jaglal Untwal, Utku Kose

*Big Data and Blockchain Technology for Secure IoT Applications*
Shitharth Selvarajan, Gouse Baig Mohammad, Sadda Bharath Reddy, Praveen Kumar Balachandran

*Technology-Based Teaching and Learning in Pakistani English Language Classrooms*
Muhammad Mooneeb Ali

*Medical Knowledge Paradigms for Enabling the Digital Health Ecosystem*
Usha Desai, Vivek P Chavda, Ankit Vijayvargiya, Ravichander Janapati

*Soft Computing in Renewable Energy Technologies*
Najib El Ouanjli, Mahmoud A. Mossa, Mariya Ouaissa, Sanjeevikumar Padmanaban, Said Mahfoud

*Leveraging the Potential of Artificial Intelligence in the Real World: Smart Cities and Healthcare*
Tien Anh Tran, Edeh Michael Onyema, Arij Naser Abougreen

*eGovernment Whole-of-Government Approach for Good Governance: The Back-Office Integrated Management IT Systems*
Said Azelmad

*Advances in Digital Marketing in the Era of Artificial Intelligence: Case Studies and Data Analysis for Business Problem Solving*
Moez Ltifi

For more information about this series, please visit: https://www.routledge.com/Advances-in-Digital-Technologies-for-Smart-Applications/book-series/ADT

# Technology-Based Teaching and Learning in Pakistani English Language Classrooms

Muhammad Mooneeb Ali

CRC Press
Taylor & Francis Group
Boca Raton  London  New York

CRC Press is an imprint of the
Taylor & Francis Group, an **informa** business

Designed cover image: © Shutterstock

First edition published 2025
by CRC Press
2385 NW Executive Center Drive, Suite 320, Boca Raton FL 33431

and by CRC Press
4 Park Square, Milton Park, Abingdon, Oxon, OX14 4RN

*CRC Press is an imprint of Taylor & Francis Group, LLC*

© 2025 Muhammad Mooneeb Ali

ISBN: 978-1-032-58589-5 (hbk)
ISBN: 978-1-032-58588-8 (pbk)
ISBN: 978-1-003-45073-3 (ebk)

DOI: 10.1201/9781003450733

Typeset in Adobe Caslon Pro
by KnowledgeWorks Global Ltd.

# Contents

CONTENTS

# 1

# INTRODUCTION

Living beings distinguish non-living beings in expression. They need it for expressing their emotions, feelings, needs, desires, likes, dislikes and much more. It is said that every living being expresses itself in its own way, and this uniqueness is due to the communication system given to them by God. Common species have a common communication system, which makes them understand each other. A dog, cat or duck can only understand the signs, communication and gestures of others. It can be said that all species share some common features in their own systems of communication. So, in other words, almost all the communication systems of living beings have some common communication features.

According to Hockett and Hockett (1960), there are certain features possessed by human beings that are distinctive from other living beings. Due to these features, the human communication system is considered a language. So, it is pivotal to view about language. Language is an amazingly diverse feature of human culture, with thousands of languages spoken around the world. There are approximately 7,000 languages spoken worldwide, although this number can vary depending on how languages are classified and what standards are used (Pereltsvaig, 2020).

Languages are usually congregated into families grounded on their ancient and operational resemblances. Some of the chief language families comprise Indo-European (which includes English, Spanish, Hindi, Russian and many others), Sino-Tibetan (including Mandarin, Cantonese and Tibetan), Afro-Asiatic (such as Arabic and Hebrew), Niger-Congo (including Swahili, Yoruba and Zulu) and Austronesian (including Malay, Tagalog and Hawaiian), among others. Many languages are endangered; that is, they are in danger of becoming extinct as there are only a few speakers who use them (Harrison, 2007).

There are some factors that contribute to language endangerment, including globalisation, cultural assimilation and government policies

DOI: 10.1201/9781003450733-1

favouring dominant languages (Lo Bianco, 2010). Languages differ in vocabulary and grammar. They are also contrastive in dialects, accents and regional variations. For example, English spoken in the United States differs in certain aspects from English spoken in the United Kingdom or Australia. Countries often have one or more official languages, which are used in government, education and official communications. For instance, Canada has two official languages, English and French, while India recognises 22 languages as scheduled languages under its constitution (Mohanty, 2006). Languages evolve over time owing to numerous factors, such as cultural changes, technological advancements and language contact. New words are coined, meanings shift and grammar rules may change. Efforts are being made to revitalise endangered languages through initiatives such as language preservation programmes, cultural education and documentation of indigenous languages.

Language has given human beings a system of communication, and with the advancement of the human race, numerous languages have arisen. These languages were initially pidgin and creole, and with acceptance and appreciation, they were utilised by a community and then society (Kachru, 1986). Moreover, some languages were initially started on the basis of race, ethnicity and religion, but later on, they were adopted by the whole community. Some of the languages used in this process died, while others became obsolete. That is why there are only a few languages in the world that have a long historical background. English is a West-Germanic language brought by the Anglo-Saxons around 500 AD (Johns, 2012). Since then, it has seen many ages and variations, but it persisted and gradually gained popularity. Presently, English has become the language of the world, and in all genres of human disciplines, English has stamped its importance. Apart from the native language, English is used as a second and foreign language, and it facilitates people of different languages to communicate with each other. Like other genres of life, in education, the value of English has elevated immensely over the last 50 years (Grigoryeva & Zakirova, 2022). Apart from the developed nations of the world, the use of English in underdeveloped countries is a mandatory element in their education system. In some of the examples of English as a second language (ESL) countries, English is mandatory till 12th grade, whereas in English as a foreign language (EFL) country, English preparatory year programmes before bachelors are a commonality (Nghia & Vu, 2023).

Leading this discussion in Southeast Asia, India and Pakistan are the two major stakeholders in this area. Let us view their brief history before moving forward.

### Brief History of Subcontinent

Subcontinent has been ruled by Muslims since the 14th century, and British people came to India in 1608 for the purpose of trade. They saw the quality, wealth, natural resources and culture and decided to increase their influence, which ended up with the War of Independence in 1857, in which the British army took over the charge of the country. Englishmen ruled the subcontinent for almost 90 years. In 1947, the subcontinent gained independence, and two nations, India and Pakistan, were formed. It is said that Englishmen went but English never. Since independence, English has been used as a language by officials and diplomats. It was appreciated by all genres of society in both countries. Various practices have been utilised to teach English at various levels (Poudel, 2022).

Pakistan is an Islamic country where English is regarded as an official language. It is the language for trade, business, governmental communication and social media. In education, English is taught as a compulsory subject till class 12. Despite having such popularity, English language learning is the biggest issue in Pakistan (Saleem, 2023). Many studies have proved that this may be due to the persistence of conventional ways of learning and teaching, which have failed to provide satisfying results (Khan, 2023). Others are of the view that Pakistan has failed to include the latest technological teaching and learning tools in education, while they have been successfully practised in advanced countries.

Then, there are serious problems with infrastructure and content. Government schools in Pakistan are somewhat satisfactory in cities as far as facilities are concerned, but in the villages, there are serious problems with proper mechanisms. Lack of resources, a deficiency of teachers and even basic facilities to shelter the students against the severity of the weather are not there. The classes are overcrowded. In a single class, usually 60–70 students are there, with only one teacher.

This teacher-student ratio is itself a troublesome factor. Due to this, a teacher cannot concentrate on every student. Also, it is difficult to manage the class. It creates suffocation, noise and health issues. Stepping ahead, one can hardly find an example across the country where an air conditioner or heater is found in a classroom. In a country where the weather is not moderate, it is hard to believe that basic facilities are not there.

English, being an official language, is rated highly in the country. It is appreciated by every member of society, and it denotes higher status. Surprisingly, there aren't many English language speakers in the country. People face trouble speaking, listening, reading and even writing English. That is why, even in any international examination, learners have to put more effort into getting a good score. The environment does not support the development of English language learning. Another very significant problem is the methods of instruction. The baseline for learning English is the grammar and translation methods used by the teacher. Also, the structure of Urdu, the native language, is opposite to English, which makes it hard to learn efficiently. The teachers have been practising techniques that have become obsolete in modern countries. These ways are unable to satiate the needs of modern learners. In this era of instant connectivity, where the internet has given people awareness, local learners are more aware of the latest things, but in the classroom, old ways are still preferred. Hence, learners become disinterested in learning or try to escape from English classrooms. Further, the syllabus is also outdated. It has failed to satiate the needs of elementary, middle and high school learners. Also, there is a huge gap between the reality a student faces outside the class and the syllabus learned inside the class. Consequently, there is a gap that is getting wider day by day, which has made overall classroom teaching and learning ineffective. There is no sign of using any technology for learning or instruction as well.

Looking at the higher education process in Pakistan, colleges are identical to schools. Even the syllabus is not impactful. Therefore, the local learner is never confident or motivated to learn and present their four skills in English. The classrooms are devoid of any tailor-made apps or tools for learning.

In universities, the conditions are a bit better. They have better infrastructure, and the student-teacher ratio is also fine. But at that level, the learners' basic language development has been completed. Also, the subjects are not developing the language; rather, they are preparing them for professional life. So, a learner can learn the basics of language. That is why learners are unable to express themselves at any job interviews or public speaking places.

The technology, even in universities, is not modern. Some good examples are there, but overall, the situation needs a change for the integration of modern technologies in classrooms. Sensitising to the situation, it is pivotal to write a book focusing on the local culture and norms inside the English language classroom. This book will focus on the inclusion of technology in English language classrooms in Pakistan. This book comprised some real-time research works regarding the employment of some technology tools in Pakistani English language classrooms.

Divided into ten chapters, this book will have practical value for people working in various domains.

This book will be helpful for teachers and students. Teachers can take some ideas from the research and implement new tools in their teaching. Students can also integrate tools for understanding English in a better way. For future researchers, policymakers and syllabus designers, this book will be valuable to properly include the latest ways in the education system of Pakistan. It will also serve as a need analysis to collect pertinent information needed for the employment of modern practices that will serve for the betterment of English language teaching and learning in Pakistan.

# 2
# TECHNOLOGY AROUND THE WORLD

Some 150 years ago, this term technology was unheard. The latest gift of science in the 20th century was the introduction of technology, which gradually entered every area of life. Since then, the rapid development of technology has changed the picture of the world. Technology has become indispensable with time. This is due to the ease and comfort it has provided to humans. Looking at the advancements of technology in the 21st century, one cannot imagine a life without technology in human society. It has become an important member of every modern-day family. If we look around us at home appliances, travel, transportation, communication methods, production and preservation of food, climate change, medicine and medical facilities, banking and corporate services, entertainment and infotainment, etc., technology is vivid everywhere (Gabriel et al., 2022).

For the use of technology, an earlier need was to develop a platform. The platform was needed to create systems that could be operated seamlessly. This platform was primarily provided by computers, and since then, the integration of technology has become faster. The latest software, applications and digital technologies have formed marvels. Furthermore, the introduction of mobile phones has opened up new avenues of learning, communication, connection and advancements in society. The revolution created by the internet has opened a new world for humans, and now learning, earning, communication, etc., are due to the internet. The use of social media websites has made people connected through photographs, videos, voice and video calls, as well as hologram technology. The world has accepted the value of technology during the COVID-19 pandemic, where everything was shifted to online. Also, it has opened a new path for entertainment. Azak et al., (2022) shared that the advent of YouTube has also provided entertainment and information with comfort.

 DOI: 10.1201/9781003450733-2

Benefits of Technology

Technology offers numerous benefits across the globe, impacting various aspects of life and society. It has revolutionised communication, enabling instant and seamless connections between individuals and communities regardless of geographical boundaries. This has facilitated an easier and faster exchange of information, nurturing global collaboration. It has transmuted academia by opening up novel learning approaches, thus enabling innovative teaching and learning methods. Online courses, educational apps and digital learning platforms have made education more accessible and personalised, empowering learners of all ages and backgrounds (Renaldo, 2022). The other benefit of technology is that it provides support for economic growth. Innovative methods for increasing productivity and creating new opportunities for businesses and entrepreneurs have helped boost the economy. It has facilitated the growth of various industries by providing ease in daily operations in production, processing and delivery. Also, the inclusion of information technology in finance and manufacturing has led to job creation (Bitto Urbanova et al., 2023).

Another addition of technology can be seen in the health sector, where it has overhauled all the previous systems. Improvements in patient care, diagnosis and treatment, telemedicine, wearable devices, electronic health records and medical imaging have enhanced access to healthcare services, thus reducing medical errors.

The development in all these sectors has improved overall efficiency in global operations. It has enabled men to maximise the optimisation of resources. Then, the use of automation, artificial intelligence (AI) and data analytics has helped organisations automate repetitive tasks and make data-driven decisions to enhance their efficiency. Then, technology has also peeped into agriculture and dairy, where various seeds, the development of crops and the yielding of agricultural and dairy products are not produced like in earlier ways. From the irrigation of fields to the production of milk, butter, meat and crops, everything has been made effective by the inclusion of technology. It has helped to double production and has also aided in reducing the issues related to these sectors. Furthermore, technology has also addressed environmental challenges and promoted sustainability. Renewable energy technologies, smart grids, energy-efficient buildings and sustainable agriculture practices are examples of how technology can contribute to mitigating climate change and preserving natural resources. Now, a lot of countries in the world are moving towards electric transportation systems due to the awareness and availability of the latest technology.

Going ahead, this world has become global due to the rapid access to information, which is a gift of technology. In this regard, no one can deny the value of the internet, which has changed everything.

Search engines and online databases have made information readily available, enabling people to educate themselves, make informed decisions and participate more actively in society. Connecting to this, some new ways of communication have also been opened, which have provided individual and community engagement. This allows individuals to connect with friends, family and like-minded individuals around the world. Social media platforms, online forums and messaging apps have enabled people to share ideas, collaborate on projects and build communities based on shared interests and values. Currently, it is technology that has a major impact on the economy of any country. The most technologically advanced countries usually have stable economies. Looking ahead, the modern world has now embarked on a new step in technology, which is AI. The use of AI has not become a commonality till now, yet developed countries have started using it in various affairs successfully. It is said that in a few years, the use of some innovative technologies like:

- Metaverse
- Non-fungible tokens (one example of NFT: If someone wants to create a work by an artist that does not exist now, i.e., burnt or destroyed, he or she will photograph it, transform it into NFT and then sell it as a digital auction.)
- Cloud computing
- Extended reality (a combination of real and virtual reality)

and many more will overhaul the patterns of human life. Furthermore, the use of AI will facilitate human beings performing all of their tasks perfectly (Ali et al., 2023).

On the other hand, technology has some pitfalls too, which are as follows:

- Humans are fearful that one day technology will replace them.

- Technology has also helped those evil minds who are creatively destructive and believe in power.
- It has served as a tool for oppression.
- The creation of new weapons, bombs, bio-bombs and viruses are also some of the most destructive examples of technology (Jang & Landuyt, 2023).

Zizek (2018), in his post-humanism theory, talked about a time when there will be human isolation. People will be together, yet they will enjoy virtual reality and virtual sex and would love to communicate virtually. So physical interaction, social connections and social collaborations will be obsolete. One can just imagine that living in one house, people will be so busy with their gadgets that they will not communicate practically. The early signs of this can be seen presently, where people have indulged themselves in mobile phones so deeply that they want to live in that virtual reality world, and they consider it better than reality. Therefore, there is a considerable decrease in the real talk time between family and friends.

Earlier, people used to send wish cards and postal letters and used to meet and greet regularly. Currently, it has been observed that everyone has gone into a shell where he or she wants to be with himself or herself and technology. Earlier E-cards and now E-messages on mobile and Emojis (E-Emotions) have created an artificial presentation of the feelings as well. One great example of this is that whenever people go to any recreational place, they focus more on taking pictures, making videos or "selfies" rather than enjoying the beauty of the place and the current moment. One believes that in an attempt to capture the scenes, people miss the beauty of the place and time.

But technology itself is not a bad thing; humans made it, and it is their duty to use it. Technology is a neutral facility; it is its use that makes it good or bad.

So, technology has become an indispensable part of modern life, driving progress, innovation and connectivity on a global scale. Its benefits extend across various sectors and have the potential to address some of the world's most pressing challenges while improving the quality of life for people around the world.

# 3

# TECHNOLOGY IN MODERN CLASSROOMS

The context, the technology and the pedagogy are the three essential components that work together harmoniously to create the modern classroom.

All three of these components have a significant role to play. These components are aimed at transforming education by the institutions, but they often fall short of expectations because one crucial component is absent. An institute might overlook pedagogy in favour of technology and a conducive learning environment. In this instance, they will probably find themselves in the "same old" scenario. The class will proceed as usual if the pedagogy isn't changed to make use of the new location and technology. It is possible that the task will be completed more quickly and comfortably, but it is unlikely that the results will change.

The proper layout, pedagogy and technology are all balanced in a modern classroom. Furthermore, a contemporary classroom needs to be set up to optimise the effects of the following four essential catalysts that are necessary to inspire students to learn: Feedback, personalisation, engagement and teamwork. The modern classroom comes to life when these elements are integrated with the three fundamental components of context, technology and pedagogy.

As an educator, one should think about how their classroom facilitates a variety of learning modalities, including whole-class instruction, collaborative teamwork, individual work, small-group work and learning outside of the classroom.

The contemporary classroom is not limited by the institute's four walls; rather, outside of the classroom, learning can be just as relevant and beneficial. Every student should be able to learn anytime, anywhere. Students require a digital environment where they can arrange all of their in-class lessons, assignments and resources in addition to their devices. The platform ought to serve as a "one-stop shop" for

DOI: 10.1201/9781003450733-3

them to use in and out of formal classrooms. School administrators can find a free digital learning platform that works with all devices and operating systems, like Class Flow, to maximise their resources.

Classrooms serve as the focal point for teaching and learning in the educational system. They are important because of their environment, role and significance in the pedagogical processes. All syllabuses and policies are made to be implemented in the classroom context. As mentioned earlier, previous classrooms were practising conventionalism. All of them had some common features, which are as follows:

- Teacher's dominance.
- Focus on memorisation.
- Learners as crammers.
- Learning tools were chalk, pens, blackboards and whiteboards.
- Overcrowded institutes.
- Drill method (Srivastava et al., 2023).

So before looking at technology in modern classrooms, let us look at some of the practices of previous classrooms from the past. Some 30–40 years ago, the classroom's ambience was extremely different from today. In developed countries, some overhead projectors (OHPs), VCDs and VCRs were available, but countries like Pakistan, India, Bangladesh and others can hardly think about them. Contrary to today, there was limited or hardly any presence of technology in the classroom. Computers were rare and often shared among students in computer labs. Furthermore, the methods of teaching relied heavily on traditional approaches such as lectures, textbooks and paper-based assignments. Interactive and multimedia learning experiences were rare; verbal instruction and printed materials were used by the teachers for conveying information. Also, some analogue tools, like chalkboards and whiteboards, were used for the visual instruction. The use of chalk and later markers for writing and drawing any content of the syllabus was a usual practice. This method is still common in underdeveloped countries. The OHPs later came into use, and they displayed transparency without any multimedia features. Going further, the classroom interactivity was below standard compared with today. Though group discussions and hands-on activities were common, there was no digital communication. Therefore, no engagement was there with multimedia content. The learners and the teachers have limited access to information. Related books, encyclopaedias and specific materials were present in libraries that were outside the classroom. Research often involved trips to the library and manual searches through card catalogues and reference books, rather than quick online searches (Tomlinson & Imbeau, 2023).

Viewing some of the assessment methods, grading of assignments and record-keeping were manual processes that were done by handwritten notes and grade books. Teachers spent significant time on paperwork, recording grades and calculating averages. This was done without the assistance of digital grading tools or online grade books. Consequently, there was limited or hardly any concept of collaboration and communication outside the classroom for learning. If there was, it was without emails, social apps and social media (Jungjohann & Gebhardt, 2023).

But with the advancement of time, technology peeped into education as well. The syllabus designers and policymakers made a gradual shift towards a new system of learning and teaching. Integrating technology was the first step towards this transformation. The earlier tools were not personally designed for learning, yet they received appreciation and provided positive results. This encouraged the policymakers to take further steps. Then, the shift towards learner-centred classrooms was observed, where the control of learning was shifted from the teacher to the learners. Conceptual learning and collaborative learning became the prominent characteristics of this new learning pattern. Teachers were not leading figures in the classrooms but facilitators. The learner was no longer focused on cramming but rather on self-paced, knowledge-based learning, which became the central point. Furthermore, teaching methods changed from GTM to communicative methods in second and foreign language contexts. This practice showed better outcomes, and the classroom ambience was changed. In the next phase, the tools for teaching and learning were also changed. It started with the inclusion of OHPs, audio and visual aids through multimedia and other pertinent devices. Since the start of the 21st century, the inclusion of the latest and most innovative technology tools has created a revolution in teaching and learning (Vitanova-Ringaceva et al., 2023).

The inception of the internet for academic purposes was a major advancement. Especially, its usage inside the classroom has changed the canvas of learning and teaching. It has also facilitated the context of learning and teaching in multiple ways. Technology tools in modern classrooms can be split into two phases, that is, pre-COVID-19 and post-COVID-19 scenarios.

Before COVID-19, classrooms were usually focused on computers, laptops, learning applications, electronic blackboards, Spectron, etc., but after COVID-19, the rigorous inclusion of mobile phones for learning and the exploitation of purposefully developed mobile apps has transformed learning and teaching methods (Bastian et al., 2023).

Modern classrooms have been shifted to the use of modern tools like (Figure 3.1)

- Kahoot
- Games
- Padlet
- Socrative
- Digital field strips and many more.

**Figure 3.1**  Modern English classrooms.

All of these learning and teaching apps have a commonality; that is, their objective is to inspire the learners towards learning. They are designed in such a way that learners do not become disinterested in learning. The use of artificial intelligence (AI) and machine learning has facilitated teachers to make tailored instructions according to the needs of the learners. Moreover, these technology tools engage learners effectively. Learning is no longer a burden for learners; rather, they take it as an interesting activity. Secondly, from the perspective of the teachers, these apps are quite helpful to support them in teaching and achieving their teaching objectives.

Now, the classroom is no longer a boring and tiresome activity; rather, it has become hybrid, flipped and even techno-personal, where personalised learning is linked with collaboration. It has also enhanced the accessibility of information for learners. Technology has simplified various complex concepts for learners. Furthermore, teachers also have to adopt this new change and equip themselves with modern methods. Now, interactive learning classrooms are the order of the day. The concept of blended learning and the inclusion of technologies have also created a vivid change in the syllabus and course materials (Ryan, 2023).

Furthermore, there is also a change in the teachers' lesson plans. So, in a nutshell, it can be said that the world has seen a shift from conventionality to modernity in education.

Apart from some positives, there are some negatives associated with technology. Some critics are of the view that the in-class exploitation of technology is a distraction, and rather than doing good, it is creating more damage to learning (Yucedal, 2023). They claim that learning is a serious process that needs attention, whereas the use of tools makes learners non-serious, and they do not achieve their objective of learning. Others believe that technology-based classrooms have empowered students and that the role of the teacher has become insignificant. Therefore, the checks and balances of the teacher are not there. Now, teachers have no importance in the classroom. The over-reliance on technology can have disadvantages, and it is feared that one day teachers will be totally replaced by technology (Kucuk, 2023). But these things need practical evidence and empirical proof. Technology has some advantages and disadvantages, and the important thing is to minimise the grey areas by controlling certain variables to achieve more benefits.

From all perspectives, the modern classroom has undergone comprehensive change, where students actively participate in creating new concepts and content in a modern classroom. They employ active learning strategies, like project-based learning and design-based learning, in which students participate in practical, pertinent and meaningful tasks.

Some exciting predictions can be made regarding technology's place in the classroom. It can be imagined that a classroom is developing into a pervasive tool that is both physically and virtually delivered and seamlessly integrated into the curriculum. Learning that happens outside of the traditional classroom will keep growing. Students, parents, teachers and employers will all be equal stakeholders in the process of making learning a lifetime endeavour. Purposefully constructed campuses will not be attractive anymore; rather, the focus will be on content and teaching. From another perspective on society, it is hoped that success gaps among the various societal classes will be minimised and that educational inequality will be lessened. So, wealth, place of birth, gender, passports and nationality will no longer be important or influential in educational outcomes. Also, while the budgets fixed on education may not rise, the number of students will, so integrating technology will enable governments to cater to a large population economically. For that, they must make better use of the resources they already have.

# 4

# TECHNOLOGY IN SUBCONTINENT CLASSROOMS

The subcontinent refers to two major countries in Asia, that is, India and Pakistan. Both share a common history. If we look 100 years ago, both countries were called subcontinent. This term, subcontinent became famous as both of them cover major areas of Asia, and it is almost a half-continent. This area was rich in various fields, and its advancement and productivity were famous around the globe. This area possesses a long history of civilisation, culture and religion. Though it was ruled by various emperors, the dynamics of this area remained the same throughout. In 1947, India and Pakistan gained their independence. As mentioned earlier, the subcontinent is a resourceful area that has a lot of stability. But surprisingly, there was no concept of formal education for everyone. Even people did not learn English for many reasons. It was Sir Sayed Ahmad Khan who gave advice to the Muslims of the subcontinent to learn English in the 19th century (Sherwani, 1944). After gaining independence, the established system of education was carried on by both countries. This system was formed by the British government. But as the government left, their teachers, curriculum designers and syllabus designers also went. This was the time when the natives joined in and started teaching the learners. As English was an important language even then, its value was appreciated amongst people. Surprisingly enough, there was no proper mechanism for learning English. Time passed, but the situation did not improve.

For the last 60 years in both countries, the education system has become predictable, with old-fashioned classrooms where even the chairs and tables are not sufficient for the sitting of learners. There are some remote areas where there are no buildings, so the teachers and

DOI: 10.1201/9781003450733-4

the students have to sit under the shade of a tree for learning. They also have to face the severity of the weather. In other scenarios, the classrooms have a blackboard with chalk for teaching. Some classrooms do not have proper electricity, fans, heaters and windows to manage the weather conditions in summer and winter (Khan et al., 2016). These are some glimpses of the physical conditions of the local classroom. Viewing the other conditions, the word technology is unheard of in most of the schools, colleges and universities across the subcontinent. There are teacher-dominated classrooms that focus on the drill method. Even in the big cities, using multimedia was considered an achievement 15 years ago (Sain, 2023).

It is said that education is changing quickly. We hear about new technological advancements every day that are changing both the world and education. Many educational technologies are essential to enhancing learning, and since these quick changes give us the chance to enhance learning at all levels, it is more crucial than ever that educators and students have access to the greatest new techniques, applications and tools available. Technology in the classroom is becoming more and more common as we move into the 21st century. Our textbooks are being replaced by technologies that allow us to explore nearly anything. Sensitising to the situation, the use of technology in classrooms across the subcontinent has undergone significant advancements in recent years, albeit with variations towards adoption and implementation amongst various regions and educational institutions. Now, educational institutions are increasingly incorporating digital learning like electronic and digital books, academic websites and multimedia content into their curricula, but they are in the initial phase. These resources provide students with access to a wealth of information and interactive learning materials, enhancing the teaching and learning experience. Resultantly, a lot of institutes in urban areas have adopted smart classroom technology, which includes interactive whiteboards, projectors and audio-visual equipment (Dahri et al., 2022). These smart classrooms facilitate dynamic and engaging teaching methods, allowing educators to deliver multimedia-rich lessons and interactive presentations. This has paved the way for online learning platforms and learning management systems (LMS). Institutes now seek to develop their own LMS to offer learners and teachers with openings for blended learning and remote education. These platforms offer features such as virtual classrooms, discussion mediums, online assessments and access to educational resources (Mujtaba Asad et al., 2022). Also, the availability of educational apps catering to various subjects and learning objectives has increased significantly. These apps cover vast topics, including language learning, mathematics, science and exam preparation, providing students with personalised learning experiences. In earlier times, there was a deficit in teachers' training programmes. Now, efforts are being made to provide teachers with academic and professional progressive opportunities to efficiently include technological practices into their teaching practices. Workshops, seminars and online courses are conducted to enhance teachers' digital literacy and pedagogical skills like other parts of the world. Also, after COVID-19, the institutions are gradually transitioning from traditional pen-and-paper assessments to digital assessments and examinations (Peled & Perzon, 2022). Online assessment tools and platforms enable educators to create, administer and evaluate assessments more efficiently while also providing instant feedback to students. On the other hand, there are some issues, like in rural areas of the subcontinent, where technology has not been used. Many schools and colleges in rural areas are focusing on previously used methods. There is also a problem of affordability amongst institutes in various areas of the subcontinent. Then there are disparities in digital literacy levels among students and teachers (Singh et al., 2021). Addressing these challenges requires concerted efforts from policymakers, educators and stakeholders. The governments are working on it, and in the last 8 years, a change has been observed in the subcontinent classrooms, where the physical conditions have improved. Moreover, the integration of modern technologies has also been added in some of the institutions, which has added a ray of hope for the creation of modern technological systems in all the classrooms across India and Pakistan. It can be said that the subcontinent classrooms are far behind in technology usage as compared to Western countries.

## Pakistani Classrooms

Pakistan is a country with a diversified culture. The first important thing is its geographical location, due to which one can see that there are different weather conditions in Pakistan. In the summer season, when the weather is extremely hot in the western part of the country, the eastern parts like Swat, Gilgit and Skardu are cold. Whereas in Karachi, the weather is usually moderate. Moreover, in the winter season, the weather becomes intense in all parts of the country, except Karachi, Hyderabad and some other areas of Sindh. Similarly, some differences exist in the local culture as well. Khyber Pakhtunkhawa's (KPs)culture is different from that of Punjab, whereas Baluchistan is different from Sindh. But all of them are united under one strong cultural tie, and that is Islamic culture. Despite the variance in culture, the classrooms in Pakistan are identical. If we look at the villages of Pakistan (in any province), we will see that they have miserable classroom facilities (Ali et al., 2024; Butt et al., 2020). The sitting facilities for the students are sometimes missing. There are instances where the classroom conditions are inappropriate. In some of the schools, there are no teachers available for teaching, whereas in others, the building is not proper. In cities and other developed areas, the conditions are much better. They have schools, colleges and universities that have basic facilities and buildings (Younas et al., 2023).

Pakistan's educational environment is characterised by linguistic diversity, with Urdu as the national language and English as the official language for education and administration. Regional languages like Punjabi, Sindhi, Pashto and Balochi are also spoken by various communities. The education system in Pakistan comprises primary, secondary and tertiary levels, with government schools, private schools and madrasas operating alongside each other, offering diverse curricula and teaching methods. The national curriculum covers subjects such as Urdu, English, mathematics, science, social studies and Islamic studies, although the implementation may vary across provinces and school types. There are a lot of challenges faced by Pakistani classrooms, including overcrowding, resource limitations, teacher shortages and unequal access to quality education, particularly in rural and marginalised areas (Ahmad et al., 2019). Efforts are being made by the administration to integrate technology into classrooms through initiatives such as smart classrooms, online platforms and digital resources to improve teaching and learning experiences, but till now, no practically comprehensive step has been taken in this regard. Another issue is the gender disparity, which has been persisting in education for a long time. Girls have to encounter obstacles like cultural norms, economic constraints and inadequate facilities, despite advancements in addressing these issues. Resultantly, a lot of females, despite their wish to study, can hardly study till 10th grade or even less. Also, some villages and areas have only primary schools, so to get a higher education, they have to go far, which is impossible. Therefore, they usually have to stop their formal education. Some initiatives are being taken for the promotion of inclusive education with the aim of accommodating diverse learning needs, including those of students with disabilities and special educational requirements, but they are lagging behind modern trends and requirements (Hussain et al., 2019). Scrutinising the teaching methods, one can see that they encompass a range of approaches, including traditional lectures, group events, project-based learning and hands-on practices, fostering critical thinking skills among students. But all these events are following previously used methods without involving the latest ways to increase the learners' interest and elevate their motivation. Furthermore, the assessment practices are also conventional and involve exams, quizzes, assignments and practical demonstrations, with ongoing enhancements to measure comprehensive learning outcomes effectively. But all these assessments are not conceptual-based; rather, they support cramming until grade 12. Therefore, learners have to face a lot of problems when they move to their graduate learning courses (Afzal & Rafiq, 2022). Looking at the teachers, there is rarely a mechanism that supports the professional development of the teacher. Around the world, it has gained primary importance, yet here, teachers are not offered any refresher courses, workshops, seminars or conferences to gain new knowledge.

Now, looking at the English language classrooms, they have teacher dominance. The control of learning, pace of learning and method of learning are all decided by the teacher in the class. He/she is considered to be the most important one in the classroom. Moreover, the teacher drives the classroom overall. The learners are quiet and pensive, and they follow instructions only (Roshin et al., 2023).

They rarely participate in classroom scenarios, and their learning is teacher-dependent. Furthermore, they are more into listening to the whole lecture and taking notes. Consequently, their participation in the classroom is very rare. For English language teaching, the Grammar Translation Method is usually used, and students follow it rigorously. In higher institutes, the drill method is utilised (Zaman & Anwar, 2023).

*Technology in Pakistani Classrooms*

In the Western world, technology has imprinted its presence, yet surprisingly, the use of modern technology in Pakistani local classrooms is still infrequent. In schools, one hardly finds technology usage, and in colleges and universities, there are instances, but they are not frequent. The technology used in colleges and universities was earlier limited to overhead projectors (OHP) and multimedia. Pakistani classrooms usually face multiple challenges related to infrastructure, resources and teaching methods. Many classrooms lacked proper lighting, ventilation and furniture. Some institutes operate in makeshift buildings. Another issue is the class size, which is often large with a single teacher teaching 70 or 80 students. Resultantly, these congested classrooms give hard times to the teachers, and they are unable to focus on each student and also find it difficult to maintain discipline (Ali et al., 2022).

The majority of the institutes lack essential educational resources such as textbooks, teaching materials and audio-visual aids. Libraries and book banks are limited. Hence, the students have limited access to reading materials and reference books. Another major problem is the traditional teaching methods, such as rote memorisation and lecture-based instruction. No emphasis is placed on interactive and student-centred learning approaches. In some areas, especially rural regions, there are significant gender disparities in access to education. Girls' schools are often underfunded and lack basic facilities, contributing to lower enrolment and attendance rates among female students. Also, some classes and families in society do not allow their females to go and study. This has created disparity among various sections of society. (Figure 4.1)

The most significant one is the integration and knowledge of technology in classrooms, which is not there across the country. Only a few institutes have access to computers, internet connectivity or audio-visual equipment. Educational technology is not

**Figure 4.1**   Pakistani classrooms.

widely used to enhance teaching and learning experiences. The lack of knowledge about technology has made it difficult to overcome the challenges of modern learners. Still, learning the difficult syllabus concept is tough, and there are many cases where a child leaves study due to a lack of understanding and comprehension, especially in English language classrooms (Farooq & Nauman, 2023). While there are many dedicated teachers, the quality of teaching varies significantly. Some teachers lack proper training and qualifications, leading to inconsistencies in teaching standards across schools. Then, socioeconomic factors, such as poverty, child labour and a lack of parental involvement, also affect the condition of classrooms.

Many students face barriers to education due to financial constraints or family obligations.

From another perspective, the most important thing about using technology in classrooms is the availability of the internet. In some of the institutes, the internet is available for the learners, whereas in others, it is available but does not provide good speed for processing and downloading; hence, it is unable to provide any support for learning. In many institutes, there is no internet facility for the learners and teachers. The other aspect is that there is an electricity shortage, and the majority of the institutes have no backup, especially the government institutes. So, it hampers the learning process. Then the content for learning is not pertinent to the use of technology. As mentioned earlier, it focuses on the drill and GTM methods. Only a few institutes bear the cost of maintaining the technology, and the institutes do not use backups for electricity to support technological tools for learning. Going ahead, there are some cultural issues as well, where the administration and teachers are adamant about using previous methods and are not prone to change. Rather, they show resistance to using technology for teaching and learning. Now, after COVID-19, a slight change has been observed where there are instances of use of technology, yet it has been restricted to only some tools (Ali et al., 2022).

Conclusively, Pakistani classrooms face numerous challenges that impact the quality of education and learning outcomes. Efforts to improve infrastructure, invest in teacher training and promote inclusive education have been made in recent years to address these issues and enhance the quality of education across the country. But still, a lot of work needs to be done in:

- Designing a proper syllabus.
- Initiating technology tools after conducting pilot studies.
- Change the mindset of the teachers and students to accept and welcome technology tools.
- Providing rigorous training to the administration to have checks and balances over the implementation of successful procedures to adopt technology.
- Encourage pertinent individuals to involve technology to get good results.

# 5
# ENGLISH LANGUAGE
# IN PAKISTAN

Since the origin of Pakistan, the English language has been considered a language for official communication. This is due to the fact that a new country decided to use English as their diplomatic language (Tuz Zahra et al., 2023). They did not use interpreters officially. The thinking of the rules prevailed in other fields and areas. All the official correspondence was written in English. Similarly, the preferred medium of instruction in the institutes was English; rather, two different mediums were formed, that is, Urdu medium schools and English medium schools, which later became English medium schools in the last decade. In the higher education system as well, English was the medium of instruction. In early times, there was some resistance to learning English due to some cultural-religious quacks, yet by the 1970s, English had become the most appreciated language amongst the citizens of the country (Ashraf, 2023).

Presently, English enjoys the status of an official language in Pakistan, and it is the language of trade, diplomacy, administration, law and commerce. It is also the language of education in various disciplines like medicine, engineering, social sciences and sciences. Furthermore, the English language enjoys high social prestige in society as well. Proficiency in English is rated higher in society. It is key to getting good positions and promotions, apart from specific knowledge (Saleem et al., 2023).

Seeing the enormous value of English, it is hard to believe that the education system does not support effective English language learning, and English language classrooms have more problems than ease (Majeed & Rehan Dar, 2022).

At the initial level, that is, primary and elementary, the base of learners is not properly geared towards English language learning. So, they face problems while learning the basics (phonetics

DOI: 10.1201/9781003450733-5

and phonology) of the English language, which later connects with the syntax of English. As Urdu is the native language, the sentence structure of Urdu is different than that of English, which can create problems in learning English. To overcome this issue, the learning method must be effective and attractive. Secondly, learning grammar is also difficult for them. Not because English grammar is complex; rather, the way of teaching English grammar is not concept-based; rather, the method is to memorise the rules. Thirdly, the acquisition of vocabulary becomes an issue sometimes for the learners.

English language classrooms commonly encounter various challenges, including inadequate curriculum, resource limitations, large class sizes, generalist teachers and instances of code-mixing and code-switching. Moreover, traditional teaching methods such as the Grammar-Translation Method (GTM) persist in schools, while colleges and universities predominantly adhere to established teacher-centred approaches, hindering students' active and autonomous learning opportunities. Emphasis on rote memorisation further exacerbates these challenges, while outdated syllabi fail to address the demands of the contemporary world. Despite attempts by administrations to mitigate these issues, the most significant challenge remains the underutilisation of technology in classrooms. While the modern world embraces technological advancements and innovative learning tools, the education sector lags behind in integrating technology effectively (Bazai et al., 2023).

In Pakistani English-language classrooms, there is a notable absence of technology integration, which is leading to a lack of access to modern learning tools. Consequently, the learning environment is characterised by ineffectiveness and disinterest among students. This deficiency persists from schools to colleges and universities, resulting in significant challenges for learners in acquiring English language skills. The absence of technological resources contributes to students' feelings of inadequacy and pressure, exacerbating their struggles with English language proficiency. Consequently, learners often fail to attain communicative competence and a comprehensive understanding of the English language, impeding the development of fundamental language skills. The incompetence reflects that they take some international tests like IELTS, GRE and Duolingo.

This situation calls for a change of mindset. It requires a shift to incorporate the latest learning methods. Now, modern learning methods dipped in the latest tools of technology are the need of the hour. These latest tools gather learners' attention and attract them towards learning. There is a dire need that, rather than feeling pressured to learn, learners should feel motivated to learn the English language, which will help to overcome academic as well as communicative issues in the country.

In response to this situation, an initiative has been taken to compile a book aimed at exploring innovative avenues for technology-driven learning in Pakistani classrooms. This book will primarily feature research-based chapters showcasing the practical application and outcomes of various technology tools in educational settings with reference to the Pakistani context. Its significance lies in providing empirical evidence and a foundational framework for administrators, policymakers, curriculum developers and content creators to understand the advantages of incorporating technology into local classrooms. Moreover, the book will serve as a catalyst for future research endeavours, inspiring the exploration of additional effective tools to modernise traditional teaching methods. For researchers, educators and students alike, this book will serve as a comprehensive guide for nurturing creativity, innovation and the implementation of novel ideas for integrating technology into local classrooms.

# 6

# INTEGRATING CELL IN PAKISTANI CLASSROOMS

Background and Some Related Studies

Tool-driven classrooms dominate modern times for the facilitation of learning and teaching. Hence, various methods have been used for the betterment and advancement of education. The internet and intranet have converted earlier ways to the latest ones. The inclusion of computers in every area of life has not only proved its importance but has also influenced modern life. Now this device (the computer) is almost part and parcel of every individual. Computers were integrated into education way back when, but they were not rigorously used in progressive nations around the world. However, in advanced countries, they were a regular member of the classroom (Kessler, 2024).

Modern computers have completely changed our communication methods. They have made it easier for us to talk to people in other countries, have video chats with anyone around the world and connect in ways we couldn't before. In schools, computers help teachers bring experts from anywhere to talk and communicate with students. Even if students can't go to faraway places like Antarctica, they can see them on a computer, talk to scientists live and go on virtual trips. This makes learning more exciting and lets students meet experts like astronauts or authors, helping them understand their lessons better.

Online learning has experienced a significant evolution, transitioning from a growing trend in the late 20th century to the primary mode of education today. Academic institutions have undergone revolutionary changes, recognising the importance of technology-mediated learning across various contexts and perspectives. The 21st century has witnessed widespread adoption of computer technologies, increasing awareness of global changes among individuals. The functionality, customisation and connectivity offered by computers have

DOI: 10.1201/9781003450733-6

made them indispensable tools for both students and teachers in the learning and teaching process (Khamitova et al., 2023)

This shift has presented opportunities for stakeholders who initially viewed it as a challenge, allowing students to leverage their technological skills effectively. Millennials now have ample opportunities to apply their tech-savvy, fuelling the growth of online learning and redirecting students' focus from recreational activities to language learning for language acquisition and cultural enrichment.

Parents, teachers, students and stakeholders have adapted to technology-mediated learning through computers. This method that uses computers for English language learning is called computer-enhanced language learning (here-on-wards CELL). CELL has already imprinted its success globally (Weng & Chiu, 2023). In the eastern part of the world, specifically in Southeast Asian countries, it is scarcely used in English-language classrooms (Sandoval-Cruz, 2022). While the approach to learning may vary across subjects, the fundamental requirements remain consistent. Foreign language acquisition (FLA) introduces unique tools, techniques and resources to enhance learning opportunities for language learners.

Some recent studies affirm the value of CELL as a modern learning method. The use of computers as supplementary material is called CELL (Ali, 2023; Ali et al., 2016). It is a multifaceted method that comes along with varied benefits. According to Abilleir and García (2021), CELL enhances language competence and boosts motivation in comparison with traditional classroom learning. The ultimate goal of any teacher is to master technology to connect with the learners. In this way, the goals can be met, and the learners can benefit from learning. Investigations performed by Fung and Deng (2024), has proved that the inclusion of technological tools is important in lifting students' motivation and learning. To make learners play an active role, the teachers need to introduce some methods for developing their interest. Second and foreign language teachers make some strategic changes to inculcate skills in their students. One of the major strategies is CELL, which inspires students to go for personalised feedback and online discussion while in the class.

Through CELL, learners can have self-learning goals and self-paced learning content. Moreover, they can understand their drawbacks and be involved in peer and group learning through CELL.

Ghory and Ghafory (2021) said that for basic English language skills, CELL can be an effective method as it can improve learners' performances with various tools.

Connecting this with the local settings in English as a second language (ESL) classes, there are several issues highlighted by various researchers. The majority of them agreed that content and methods of teaching need revamping (Masood et al., 2021). As CELL has been utilised on various continents and nations, it can be beneficial for local learners as well. While some other scholars pointed out some other significant factors that contributed to the success of CELL. They think that CELL creates learning interactions that can be done through the utilisation of apps and software. This helps to engage learners. Li (2023) stated that learning stimulations are developed through apps, which makes learning more stress-free and comfortable. Even the most complex concepts are learned with ease. Further, software and apps are designed to help humans retain knowledge. Computers also help to improve confidence levels and participation in learning, which creates a positive environment (Bahari et al., 2023). English as a second language has always been a tough road for L2 learners. Specifically, in Asia, English language learning contexts are not giving wishful results (Kaur et al., 2023). Various methods have been used for this purpose with a minimum outcome. With the rapid change in various dimensions of the world, these L2 learners find themselves having difficulty expressing and communicating in the English language. For this purpose, researchers are keen to employ unique methods to improve their productivity in English language learning. Alsuhaibani (2019) views CELL as providing expediency in the learning process. It can offer remote learning, and the pace of the learning can be controlled by the learners, not the teachers. In this way, it is contrary to the already used methods. Going ahead, in current times, digital education has been given much importance, so CELL can help to structure critical thinking, solve problems and develop minds with technology. It also helps to increase communication through collaboration. Shadiev and Liang (2024) advocated that CELL platforms foster collaboration through virtual learning, video-based learning and online classrooms. Moreover, it also helps to provide personalised feedback by tracking the performance and customised paths of learning to manage the needs of learners.

CELL also provides convenience and flexibility in learning in connection with location and timing. Now learners can learn from home while sitting at their personal computers at their desired time (In this way, learning becomes accessible for every learner. Further, the inclusion of multimedia features like animations, video, audio and interactive learning platforms also evokes learning and engagement. It develops their comprehension and improves their digital knowledge, which is pivotal in the modern era (Yang et al., 2022). Then CELL is a cost-saving method as it minimises physical material issues and permits online solutions to learning.

There are several advantages outlined by various scholars regarding the use of computers in education. Taghizadeh and Hasani Yourdshahi (2020) shared that computers are the tools for accessing information instantly as they have internet. They permit their users to explore their desired aspects globally. The diversity offered by computers on topics is indeed appreciable and not possible humanly (Sabiri, 2020).

On the other hand, there are some disadvantages to this method as well. Sometimes technical glitches can be an issue, which can create frustration for learners (Park & Son, 2022). Malfunction issues and internet connectivity problems can create hindrances in the process of learning.

Some learners cannot have access to digital resources, which creates inequality in accessing CELL opportunities. Another problem can be the overdependence on technology. Excessive use of CELL tools may create social interaction problems where learners are not feasible in real classroom situations and they become impatient in getting feedback (Mertala, 2019). Then, the security and privacy of data can also be breached, which is common in the digital world. This may lead to the leak of personalised information.

In a nutshell, CELL has some disadvantages, but it has more advantages, and it is its use that determines its value. It is important to create a balance between learning through technology and orthodox methods.

Looking at some studies for referencing, Alzu'bi (2023) examined the impact of a software program (paragraph Punch) on the writing abilities of learners. The sample size was 80, which was placed in equal numbers in two clusters of 40 each (an experiment and a controlled bunch of learners). One group was taught in an already-practised way, while the other used a computer-assisted language learning (CALL) platform through software. Later, by applying the *t*-test, the data were examined to scrutinise the result. The conclusions drawn supported the effectiveness of CELL and claimed that it strongly influences the learners' writing abilities. They also claim it to be an alternative way of uplifting writing.

Arvand and Gorjian (2022), in the context of CALL, performed exploration to view the infrastructural demands of applying CELL in the class. In the study, data from the university teachers were collected. Through a random sample collection method, the data were collected through a questionnaire. The K-S test was executed and applied for the extraction of the results. The outcomes mirrored the fact that CELL is a pivotal method. An exploration to view the value of CELL can be enhanced if some chief facilities can be added to the classrooms. They also shared that running CELL classes effectively demands basic technological infrastructure.

Çakmak (2022) performed an enquiry regarding the active involvement of the learners in a digital ambience in COVID-19 scenarios. Their aim was to deeply bifurcate the effectiveness of video classes and online classes through CELL. The learners were one hundred who were registered in the spring 2022 semester and were studying online by video and in live classes. Almost half of them studied online, whereas half of them studied by watching videos. When data were collected and results were drawn, the researcher viewed the significant value and impact of using the live class method, which made learners interactive, active and better performers in contrast to those who learned by watching videos only. This research reflects that choosing the right platform for learning under the CELL method is quite pivotal in digital education.

Abbasi et al. (2024) studied computer mediation in English as a foreign language (EFL) classrooms, which have different dynamics from ESL compulsory classrooms. Initially, a questionnaire was made and set to be answered by 26 serving teachers. In a qualitative way, the results were examined, and it was concluded that teachers were passionate about teaching through computers. They said that computer-mediated learning and teaching can have advantages in higher education in Pakistan. Likewise, Aziz and Hamzah (2020), in their research, explored the beliefs of EFL teachers and, by a qualitative method, collected data from 150 teachers in Okara (a district of Punjab, Pakistan). Their study was different as they explored the issues and challenges of novel teachers using computers in EFL classrooms. They shared multiple problems being faced by local instructors due to a lack of basic facilities in their pedagogical contexts. They suggested enhancing the classrooms' ambience, facilities and infrastructure in order to use computers for learning. Budiana (2021) shared in his research about the opinions of learners on using computers in English classrooms in listening contexts. They shared that learners were comfortable and relaxed while using computers for listening in their learning. It was also shared that for the development of any language skill, the use of computers is encouraged.

### Theoretical Construct

From a variety of theories used for the acceptance of technology, the Unified Theory of Acceptance and Use of Technology (UTAUT) has been chosen for this study. UTAUT is a significant theoretical model proposed by Venkatesh et al. (2003). It is crucial for understanding user acceptance and behaviour towards technology (Akinnuwesi et al., 2022). UTAUT also considers attitude towards technology use, self-efficacy and anxiety as indirect determinants of intention. Moreover, the model incorporates moderators like gender, age, voluntariness and experience to refine the understanding of how intention and behaviour evolve over time (Ustun et al., 2023). In comparison, both the Technology Acceptance Model (TAM) and UTAUT highlight the importance of behavioural intention in determining actual technology use. TAM focuses on attitudes towards technology use, shaped by perceived usefulness and perceived ease of use, influenced by various external factors. UTAUT extends TAM by integrating four constructs – performance expectancy, effort expectancy, social influence and facilitating conditions – to predict usage intention. Moderators such as age, gender, experience and voluntariness further mediate the impact of these constructs on intention (Bajunaied & Kamarudin, 2023). (Figure 6.1)

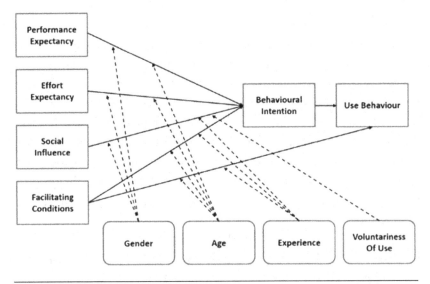

**Figure 6.1**    UTAUT model. (Vankatesh et al., 2003).

The above-mentioned model shows that technology consumption is controlled by behaviour. This supposed probability of technology acceptance and adaptation relies on the direct impact of the following four pivotal constructs:

- Expectancy of performance (performance expectancy)
- Expectancy of effort (effort expectancy)
- Society's influence (social influence)
- Facilitating situations (facility conditions)

The predictors' effect is toned down by age, gender, experience and willingness to use the technology (Venkatesh et al., 2003).

While TAM and UTAUT have been extensively utilised in management information systems (MIS) and biomedical informatics, criticisms have been raised regarding their limitations. This theory is also widely used to explore the acceptance of any new technology in the current era. With the rapid development, innovation and production of various technologies, this theory has become the most significant one in modern times in comprehending people's behaviours towards technology.

Relevant Research on UTAUT

Attuquayefio and Addo (2014), in their research, employed UTAUT to determine the predictor power of the intentions of the learners for the use and acceptance of information and communication technologies (ICT). Four hundred learners were made part of the study belonging to the arts and business faculties. The outcomes revealed that the intention of the learners was predicted positively, and their behaviour towards the use of ICT was also positive. The studies revealed that more studies should be conducted to use UTAUT, and they found this theory pertinent to investigating behaviours regarding the use of any technology.

Wu et al. (2022) studied the willingness of college students towards artificial intelligence (AI) and the AI-supported learning context. This research was based on UTAT and followed the constructs of the UTAUT theory rigorously. The outcomes of this study showed that the expectancy of effort, the expectancy of performance and the social impact all have a positive relationship with each other. This study can be beneficial for constructing a quality AI-mediated environment amongst the learners. Finally, a study by Almetere et al. (2020) reviewed the factors influencing the adaptation of internet of things (IoT) technology in an educational context. The learners were undergraduates from public-sector universities in Saudi Arabia. Like the other studies, the framework here is UTAUT. Through a questionnaire, they explored the constructs of the theory, which are expectancy in performance, expectancy in effort, societal influence and facility conditions. Through these constructs, they found out that learners were ready to use IOT for their learning affairs. They also validated that all the constructs were found to be positively influencing the predictors. All these studies reflect that CELL has imprinted its value splendidly. However, these studies also created a research gap, which led us to the decision to conduct a study in the local context. Earlier studies are rare, but one can seldom look at a comprehensive investigation that looks at the mindsets and perceptions of two imperative educational figures, that is, tutors and students. Therefore, this study will be important as it will perform an experiment to look at the value of CELL in the

Pakistani setting. This work will open up new doors of awareness and understanding.

### Objectives of This Study

It has already been discussed in Chapter 4 that classrooms in Southeast Asia are not technology-oriented. They follow conventionality. Now, if one looks specifically at Pakistani classrooms, they are following previously used ways for teaching and learning. Sensitising to the situation, the objectives for this section will be as follows:

- To collect the opinions of the teachers apropos the incorporation of CELL in ESL classes.
- To gather the opinions of learners towards CELL's integration in their classrooms.

### Research Questions

- What views do students hold about CELL as a learning method?
- What views do instructors have about CELL's inclusion in their classes?

### Methodology

This research mixes quantitative and qualitative methods. Initially, to interpret learners' data, the quantitative method was used, whereas for interpreting teachers' data, the qualitative method was used. The tool for collecting data from learners was a questionnaire, in which the interviews conducted were later presented through descriptive analysis. Moreover, the tool for teachers was interviews with open-ended questions, which were later transcribed and analysed using a content analysis method. A mixed-method approach is beneficial for a comprehensive study of a particular area or point. Initially, the learners' opinions are presented below, and after the findings and discussion, teachers' experiences are scripted.

Some important variables in this study were managed to maintain the research's validity. The age and gender, social-cultural background and ethnicity of the learners were identical. Further, the economic background and technology knowledge were also similar. This was performed to create a valid population for the research. Secondly, for the teachers, all the teachers were regulars with over 10 years' experience. All of them were males and aged between 40 and 45. All of them were proficient in using technology generally.

## Results

In this section, Tables 6.1–6.10 show the results of students' opinions about CELL.

*Statistics of Validity and Reliability*

*No: Means number*
  *P: Means percentage*
  1. Summary of case processed.

**Table 6.1**   Validity Statistics

| NO. OF PARTICIPANTS | VALIDITY | 100 | 100.0 |
|---|---|---|---|
| | Exclude | 0 | .0 |
| | Overall | 100 | 100.0 |
| | | No: | P |
| Summary of the case processed | | | |

No of participants validity
2. Statistics of reliability.

**Table 6.2**   Reliability Statistics

| RELIABILITY STATISTICS OF RELIABILITY | |
|---|---|
| CRONBACH ALPHA | ITEM NO. |
| .715 | 5 |

The statistical presentation of Cronbach's alpha value of .715 in Table 6.2 asserts that the questionnaire is valid and also reliable.

*Questionnaire Tables Regarding Frequency Measurement*

## Q.1. Do you think CELL motivates you to learn?

**Table 6.3**   Responses of the participants on Likert Scale

| VALID | FRQ | P | V.P. | C.P. |
|---|---|---|---|---|
| S. Disagree | 5 | 5.0 | 5.0 | 5.0 |
| Disagree | 5 | 5.0 | 5.0 | 10.0 |
| Neutral | 10 | 10.0 | 10.0 | 20.0 |
| Agree | 35 | 35.0 | 35 | 55.0 |
| Strongly agree | 45 | 45.0 | 45.0 | 100 |
| Total | 100 | 100.0 | 100.0 | |

The data presented in Table 6.3 in the form of frequencies indicate that students feel motivation while applying CELL in their learning. The majority of learners felt it as an element of motivation that urges them to take a vibrant part in learning domains. Very few learners felt no motivation to use CELL. The cumulative percentage is also on the higher side.

## Q.2. Did you find it a boring learning method?

**Table 6.4**   Responses of the participants on Likert Scale

| VALID | FRQ | P | V.P. | C.P. |
|---|---|---|---|---|
| S. Disagree | 35 | 35.0 | 35.0 | 35.0 |
| Disagree | 40 | 40.0 | 40.0 | 75.0 |
| Neutral | 15 | 15.0 | 15.0 | 90.0 |
| Agree | 5 | 5.0 | 5.0 | 95.0 |
| S. Agree | 5 | 5.0 | 5.0 | 100.0 |
| Total | 100 | 100.0 | 100.0 | |

The figures in the above-mentioned data reveal that learners find CELL as an interesting method for their learning. The students' replies show that they do not agree with the question, and hence the majority either strongly opposed or disagreed. This exhibits the vitality of CELL and authenticates that it is a stimulating method that encourages the learners towards learning with a positive frame of mind.

### Q.3. Is CELL better than earlier practised method?

**Table 6.5**   Responses of the participants on Likert Scale

| VALID | FRQ | P | V.P. | C.P. |
|---|---|---|---|---|
| S. Disagree | 5 | 5.0 | 5.0 | 5.0 |
| Disagree | 5 | 5.0 | 5.0 | 10.0 |
| Neutral | 5 | 5.0 | 5.0 | 15.0 |
| Agree | 30 | 30.0 | 30.0 | 45.0 |
| Strongly agree | 55 | 55.0 | 55.0 | 100.0 |
| Total | 100 | 100.0 | 100.0 | |

The frequencies presented here are reflecting the learners' opinions. They clearly said that CELL is an effective way of learning in comparison with already used learning ways. Looking at the values, 85% of learners are in support of this statement of the question and only 10% oppose it. This also echoes that CELL has developed its reputation higher in comparison with the earlier methods and learners liked it.

### Q.4. Does CELL divert your learning?

**Table 6.6**   Responses of the participants on Likert Scale

| VALID | FRQ | P | V.P. | C.P. |
|---|---|---|---|---|
| S. Disagree | 45 | 45.0 | 45.0 | 45.0 |
| Disagree | 35 | 35.0 | 35.0 | 80.0 |
| Neutral | 10 | 10.0 | 10.0 | 90.0 |
| Agree | 5 | 5.0 | 5.0 | 95.0 |
| Strongly agree | 5 | 5.0 | 5.0 | 100.0 |
| Total | 100 | 100.0 | 100.0 | |

Students in this question shared that they did not experience any diversion in their learning or felt distracted. Here, 80% of students differ from the question. It dominatingly presents that CELL develops an interest in learning and improves concentration levels rather than creating any deviation in learning procedures.

## Q.5. Does CELL provide innovative learning ways?

**Table 6.7**  Responses of the participants on Likert Scale

|  | FRQ | P | V.P. | C.P. |
|---|---|---|---|---|
| Valid S. Disagree | 5 | 5.0 | 5.0 | 5.0 |
| Disagree | 5 | 5.0 | 5.0 | 10.0 |
| Neutral | 10 | 10.0 | 10.0 | 20.0 |
| Agree | 40 | 40.0 | 40.0 | 60.0 |
| Strongly agree | 40 | 40.0 | 40.0 | 100.0 |
| Total | 100 | 100.0 | 100.0 | |

In this question, the replies mirror the opinions. A huge percentage of learners agreed that CELL truly gives the latest and innovative learning situations. Not only does it have variety, but every aspect of CELL is appealing and effective to make learning a productive process.

## Q.6. Do you think it develops interest towards learning?

**Table 6.8**  Responses of the participants on Likert Scale

|  | FRQ | P | V.P. | C.P. |
|---|---|---|---|---|
| Valid S. Disagree | 3 | 3.0 | 3.0 | 3.0 |
| Disagree | 2 | 2.0 | 2.0 | 5.0 |
| Neutral | 5 | 5.0 | 5.0 | 10.0 |
| Agree | 45 | 45.0 | 45.0 | 55.0 |
| Strongly agree | 45 | 45.0 | 45.0 | 100.0 |
| Total | 100 | 100.0 | 100.0 | |

In this question, the learners supported the view that CELL develops their interest in learning. The values of frequencies show that CELL not only creates interest in the learners, but it also has some influence that increases their concentration level. The values show that most learners agreed with this question.

## Q.7. Does it promote independence in learning?

**Table 6.9**  Responses of the participants on Likert Scale

|  | FRQ | P | V.P. | C.P. |
|---|---|---|---|---|
| Valid S. Disagree | 7 | 7.0 | 7.0 | 7.0 |
| Disagree | 3 | 3.0 | 3.0 | 10.0 |
| Neutral | 3 | 3.0 | 3.0 | 13.0 |
| Agree | 37 | 37.0 | 37.0 | 50.3 |
| Strongly Agree | 50 | 50.0 | 50.0 | 100.0 |
| Total | 100 | 100.0 | 100.0 | |

The values show that learners viewed CELL as a dominating way to make learners self-sufficient. Majorly the participants favour this question. They agree with the view that they feel freedom in learning. This can be a distinctive aspect of CELL in comparison with their previous learning ways.

### Q.8. Does it offer personalised learning situations?

Table 6.10   Responses of the participants on Likert Scale

|                    | FRQ | P     | V.P.  | C.P.  |
|--------------------|-----|-------|-------|-------|
| Valid S. Disagree  | 3   | 3.0   | 3.0   | 3.0   |
| Disagree           | 7   | 7.0   | 7.0   | 10.0  |
| Neutral            | 10  | 10.0  | 10.0  | 20.0  |
| Agree              | 43  | 43.0  | 43.0  | 63.3  |
| Strongly agree     | 40  | 40.0  | 40.0  | 100.0 |
| Total              | 100 | 100.0 | 100.0 |       |

These values show that CELL is a method that makes learning individual and personalised. The learners' opinion is presented through frequencies. The majority of learners said that CELL develops personalisation in learning ventures. In this way, the learners can integrate their own ideas and develop their own learning sense. In a nutshell, they can develop their own learning strip.

### Findings

The percentages of the frequencies in every question give clear results that students' perception regarding CELL is positive and they have shown confidence in this new method. If we look at all the questions, there are only a few learners who either opposed this method or were confused about the implementation of CELL in their learning. The extractions made from these results validate that CELL can be implemented in local classes for English learning. Further, some of the questions' replies also validated that CELL motivates learners. It also develops independence in learning and personalisation. Thus, the findings extracted here show that learners had a wonderful experience while using CELL in learning.

## Discussion

This section presents the discussion of learners' views regarding CELL. The questions asked from everyone were written in a simple language to help learners comprehend the meaning. In all the questions, the percentage of neutrals is quite low, indicating that the learners who experienced CELL were pretty clear about its utility. Moreover. The findings taken from the results tie up with the study by Alotaibi and Alzu'bi (2022), who were of the view that computers have been found to be an interesting and important ingredient in modern classrooms. The integration of this method amalgamates the advanced technology of computers into language teaching and learning in this research, which makes the learning process much easier and more fruitful. Further, the motivation provided to the learners here is also explained by some other researchers (Arvand & Gorjian, 2022), who were of the view that involving computers will add motivation and develop interest amongst students. Further, the results also ascertain that independence and personalisation in learning are pivotal. This is also stressed by Çakmak (2022), who viewed the integration of CELL as a source of providing freedom and personalisation to learners in their affairs of learning. Overall, the learners found CELL to be a more impactful, interesting and effective method in comparison with the already-practised method. In a nutshell, these perspectives can be beneficial for future researchers, and researchers can exploit CELL as their main source of teaching English.

Eyeing the findings from the UTAUT theory perspective, this section justifies the important constructs of this theory.

UTAUT theory talks about the attitudes of the participants towards the use of any technology. Here we can see that the presentation of data is aptly determining the attitude of the learners, and they have registered their opinion against each question. Moreover, the next significant point is about self-efficacy. In this research, this is also justified as CELL creates an ambience that leads learners to have self-confidence in doing tasks individually without the support of a teacher. Moreover, the satisfaction of the learners also raises their expectations for their performance. Further, anxiety is not present in CELL classrooms, as they offer various interestingly intuitive activities for learners. Also, social influence can be seen in this research, where the learners believed that integrating technology was the need of the hour. Overall, the research's section connects with the UTAUT theory, where the learners were willing to adopt this method for learning positively.

### Teachers Interviews

As mentioned in the methodology, for collecting the opinions of the teachers' interviews, open-ended questions were conducted. The interviews were recorded with their consent. From the transcription of the interviews, content analysis was performed as key themes were taken out, and then transcription was done. Further, from the transcription of the interviews, content analysis was performed as key themes were taken out. Finally, the results were extracted.

### *Theme I*

This is the first theme that talks about the implementation of CELL in the teaching process. The teachers discussed their thoughts vividly. They were of the view that CELL has currently captured education in a positive way, and its implementation is novel and can be an effective way to increase motivation for learners. Further, they were of the view that adding a technology tool would bring a new wave of modernity to the classroom, where the atmosphere would be more positive.

Teacher 1 has shared:

> CELL is a new method for my classroom, rather than in our education system. After exploiting it, I concluded that it can comprehensively change the atmosphere of my class. It facilitated me perfectly, and the learners were also taking an interest.

Teacher 3 expressed:

> I found it interesting and attractively impactful for me and the learners. I shifted my blackboard activities to the CELL method, and the results were amazing. I feel it should be part of my teaching methodology.

*Theme II*

This theme represents the view that teachers who participated in the experimental process felt insecure about using CELL or not. The teachers shared that, though it was the first time they used CELL for teaching, it helped them a lot. This method was supportive and riveting. During the whole process of the experiment, they did not feel that, at any stage, their position as a teacher was under threat. They admitted that though their role had changed, their presence and value became higher. Moreover, this new role of technology and syllabus facilitator was more appealing to them.

In the teacher's seven expressions:

> I don't see CELL as a threat to my position. Rather, I would say that it added support to my teaching. Yes, I would agree that I had to mold my teaching technique to make learners able to take charge of the classroom, yet I knew that from lesson planning to the organization and conduct of the class, each step was designed and led by me. I found CELL a perfect learning companion.

Teacher 5 said:

> "CELL has been an outstanding experience, and I think it will never be a threat to any teacher. In fact, it will be an effective companion for English language teachers to perform their language tasks comfortably".

*Theme III*

The third theme talks about the view that was CELL helpful for them in teaching. The teacher expressed that CELL activities and involvement were both notable. Not only did CELL help to increase the learning efficiency of the learner, but it also helped teachers achieve their objectives effectively.

Teacher 8 said:

> I think it elevated my performance and supported me to achieve my teaching goals. By encouraging learners to follow my instructions, the path became easy without any predicaments. Also, the connection between learners and learning became stronger.

Teacher 10 shared:

Indeed, it gave me proper help to achieve my learning objectives. I would recommend the use of CELL to everyone. The impactful integration of this tool has given me a space to implement my lesson as per my plan.

*Theme IV*

The fourth theme presents whether CELL is advantageous for learning or not. All the teachers recommended the implementation of CELL by expressing that it was a novel and magnificent experience to implement CELL in their teaching affairs. They believed that CELL provides a lot of benefits, like audio and visual facilities, different learning paths, some attractive activities and some fun types of learning to attract viewers and learners.

Teacher 7 has presented:

My viewpoint will strongly support the use of CELL. This method is extremely useful and prolific. I found in it some variety, attraction, and productivity for me and my learners.

Teacher 10 shared:

Well, CELL is perfectly apt for learning. Our English language classrooms needed some novelty, and I am happy that CELL has provided that by presenting some unknown, unheard, and unused ways that are not only catchy but also easy to understand and adopt.

*Theme V*

This theme discusses some features or hallmark elements of the CELL. The teachers shared varied features of CELL according to their experience. Some believed that its impact lies in its variety, whereas others viewed CELL as providing ease and comfort to the learners. In total, everyone agreed that CELL has given them benefits in their teaching affairs.

Teacher 8 shared:

I guess! CELL has unlimited benefits. The learning software, creativity and innovation, interesting methods, and attraction all had a deep impact on me and my students. I believe it has more benefits than issues.

Teacher 4 said:

If I look at what I experience having CELL inside my classroom, I cannot count the benefits. They are unlimited. It comes up with a lot of variety that supports learners in learning. Secondly, it also helps to fill in the differences in learning amongst my students and supports all of them to learn collectively as well.

## Findings .

Here, all the answers have been collected from the recordings, which were later transcribed. Further, content analysis was done, and some themes were developed. Under each theme, some of the relevant replies have been recorded. In seeing all the themes, the replies of the teachers have been presented randomly to cover things comprehensively. The teachers shared the benefits of CELL. They also questioned some features of this method and whether it was a threat to them or not. The teachers said that CELL is a process of support and assistance that eases their teaching methods and provides help in learning and teaching. They also shared that CELL was interesting enough to help them achieve their goals and objectives. From the findings, it can be inferred that CELL is appreciated by the teachers for being a major tool and method in their classes.

## Discussion

This study provides awareness of the perspectives held by teachers in Pakistan towards CELL. In a linguistic diversity where a lot of languages are spoken sometimes, it becomes difficult for the learners to achieve mastery in more than one language. This is the precise situation in Pakistani classrooms where English is a second language. So, involving a new method can be interesting for determining its efficacy. The opinions recorded from this research validated that even the new users of this method felt comfortable while using it. This is also said by Abbasi et al. (2024), who shared by saying that CELL simplifies teachers teaching procedures. Further, it also enables them to manage the classrooms. Also, the results from the views of teachers share that there are varied learning temperaments of learners inside the classroom, so teaching them the same syllabus has been a problem and may be one of the reasons learners do not take an interest in learning. The integral point of CELL is the personalised learning style, which makes learning contextual and allows individuals to develop their interest in learning. This gradually helps the teacher get positive results. This is also shared by Ghory and Ghafory (2021), who looked at CELL as a way to encourage personalisation in learning affairs. Overall, the results of this section tie up with the conclusions of Shadiev et al. (2023), who saw CELL as a modern approach to increasing the effectiveness and efficiency of learning and teachers. Finally, this study also joins the findings of Li (2023), who researched that CELL strongly impacts classrooms that are conservative, that is, using paper, pencil, chalk and a blackboard for learning. Su et al.,(2021) stated that CALL is a vibrant, interdisciplinary subject with expanding research potential and topic diversity because of the development of digital devices.

The perspective of the teachers shows that CELL is a quality way of learning the English language with new techniques and paths. The opinions of the instructors also reflect a lot of benefits, and thus it validates that CELL is not a technique but rather a complete learning method that encompasses techniques, ways and processes to enhance English learning.

Viewing the results from the UTAUT theory's lens; from both learners' and instructors' perspectives, it can be said that this research aptly justifies the constructs of the UTAUT theory. Firstly, the learners and the instructors were both satisfied with the use of this new technology. It can be seen that the positive attitude was reflected in the questionnaires of the learners and the teachers. This is related to the expected performance of the UTAT theory. This is also connected to the research by Attuquayefio and Addo (2014), who concluded that the behaviours of the learners were not anxious and that external factors like social influence and facility conditions were found to be advantageous for learning through technology.

Also, the willingness of the instructors and the students here is relevant to the UTAUT theory, which has augmented that learners' willingness is pivotal as it paves the way for better performance. This is aligned with the study by Wu et al. (2022), who showed that the willingness of learners in an AI context is significantly important in increasing their performance.

Another important thing found in this study was that the reflection of the answer showed that the intentions of learners and instructors were not negative regarding CELL. They appreciated this new way of handling their affairs and were ready to adopt it. This was also advocated by Almetere et al. (2020), who viewed intentions as predictors that decide the acceptance or rejection of any technology for learning.

## Conclusion

Overall, this chapter showed some interesting aspects of using CELL in English-language classrooms. The overall findings and discussion supported the use of CELL. The two chief constituents of the classroom, that is, learners and instructors, both showed positive views about CELL. Both teachers and students also felt motivated and happy to give value to this new method in their already established learning ways. This has provided a basis for the use of CELL in the local classrooms for effective consequences. In a country where there is a teacher shortage and sometimes infrastructure and buildings are not there, CELL can be a good alternative for total online classes. Even in hilly areas where, due to extreme weather conditions, it is difficult for the kids to move freely in extreme seasons, CELL can provide the best alternative. Conclusively, CELL, along with its varied advantages, can prove beneficial for the local classroom, and it can cover up a lot of problems and deficiencies in learning and teaching.

Finally, these results can also provide direction to content developers in Pakistan. They can develop content that supports CELL activities and encourages the institutes to consider its utility and implementation.

## Recommendations

Based on the findings gathered from learners' and instructors' opinions, some recommendations are as follows:

- CELL should be introduced for English language learning by the curriculum designers.
- CELL must be a regular part of the classroom.

- The institute's administration should be given guidance on how to use CELL.
- Institute heads should be given freedom and encouragement to exploit CELL.
- Teacher seminars should be done to introduce this method comprehensively.
- Learners should also be given motivation to use CELL.

### Students' Questionnaire

1. Do you think CELL motivates you to learn?
2. Did you find it a boring learning method?
3. Is CELL better than earlier practised method?
4. Does CELL divert your learning?
5. Does CELL provide innovative learning ways?
6. Do you think it develops interest towards learning?
7. Does it promote independence in learning?
8. Does it offer personalised learning situations?

### Teachers' Questionnaire

1. What do you think about the implementation of CELL?
2. Is it a threat to your position inside the class?
3. Do you think CELL helped you to achieve your teaching objectives?
4. Do you think it is beneficial for learning?
5. Do you think there are some hallmarks of CELL?

This research is a mixture of quantitative and qualitative methods. Initially, to interpret learners' data, the quantitative method was used, whereas for interpreting teachers' data, the qualitative method was used. The tool for collecting data from learners was a questionnaire, in which the interviews conducted were later presented through descriptive analysis. Moreover, the tool for teachers was interviews with open-ended questions, which were later transcribed and analysed using a content analysis method. This study states that a mixed-methods approach is beneficial for a comprehensive study of a particular area or point. Initially, the learners' opinions are presented below, and after the findings and discussion, teachers' experiences are scripted.

Some important variables in this study were managed to maintain the research's validity, that is, age and gender, social-cultural background and ethnicity of the learners. Further, the economic background and technology knowledge were also similar. This was performed to create a valid population for the research. Secondly, for the teachers, all the teachers were regulars with over 10 years' experience. All of them were males and aged between 40 and 45. All of them were proficient in using technology generally.

# 7

# THE APPLICATION OF CELL IN RURAL ENGLISH LANGUAGE CLASSROOMS

### Background and Some Related Studies

Pakistan, being a diverse country, has multiple languages and eth-
nicities. It boasts a rich linguistic landscape, having more than 60
languages spoken around the country (Rahman, 2006). Despite Urdu
being the state language, English holds a dominant position in various spheres of power, such as administration, judiciary, military, education and media. This prominence of English is seen as a pathway to
community and financial advancement, honour and status in Pakistan
(Capstick, 2019; Shamim, 2011), making it crucial for securing
employment in both the public and private sectors (Channa, 2017).

Furthermore, English language teaching has been one of the major
subjects in classrooms in English as a second language (ESL) countries.
In Pakistan, English has been taught as a mandatory subject since grade 1.
Till high school, it is included in their syllabus as a compulsion. Owing to
the value of the language, it is also given importance by parents, society,
teachers and academia. Therefore, the instruction and learning of English
hold high discussion in the educational system (Codó & Riera-Gil, 2022).
Having such importance amongst people, English language learning is an
area of trouble for local students. Learning by previous practices like chalk
and a blackboard supported by either the grammar-translation method
or the rote learning method, the results are not satisfactory. Therefore,
students want to escape from English learning. The worrying element is
that this is the same for basic English language skills (Fan, 2023). One
prominent issue while learning English is the class sizes in Pakistan,
which has more than 70 students in one classroom (Ahmad et al., 2020),
which is a global issue as well This makes it problematic for instructors
to implement learner-dominant teaching methods or conduct group

DOI: 10.1201/9781003450733-7

performances (Hossain & Haque, 2022). Additionally, handling learners, particularly during speaking events, becomes challenging in large classes (Teachers also face challenges related to the availability and capital for having any resources, particularly in rural institutes (Hungi et al., 2017). While multimedia technology is recognised as a useful tool for learning English (Yasin et al., 2021), its accessibility in Pakistani schools remains limited (Nawab, 2017). Another key issue is the low proficiency and confidence levels of teachers in English speaking (Ahn, 2014;), leading them to use Urdu or local languages as mediums of instruction due to their own language competence issues (Coleman, 2010). This language barrier also affects communication and comprehension between teachers and students, especially in rural areas (Akram, 2017;). Moreover, motivating learners, especially in rural settings, is a challenge as they struggle to see the practical application of English in their lives (Incorporating creative activities into the curriculum is suggested as a way to enhance learner motivation (A lot of people, when attempting foreign tests, are unsuccessful in getting their desired results as their basic language skills are not refined.

Since independence till 2010, Urdu and English medium systems were rigorously followed in the country; yet, after the decision in the National Assembly through Amendment (18th), a slight change has occurred with schools and colleges being English-only (Asif et al., 2020). Budiana (2021) said that the modern classroom supports the English language to enable learners to learn various skills needed for progress. This amendment is theoretically perfect, but there are a lot of issues with its practical implementation. The major issues come in rural educational institutes, where there are some obstacles like

- Old-fashioned teaching.
- Learners are not energetic towards e-learning.
- Management is not concerned with the latest methods of e-learning.
- Modern resources are not encouraged (Halai & Durrani, 2021).

Apart from that, some other issues are as follows:

- Lack of teachers.
- Lack of classroom facilities.
- Unrealistic course and syllabus designs (Bangash & Haq, 2021).

Due to all of these problems, the learners develop negative attitudes towards learning the English language. Akram et al. (2020) are of the opinion that language attitudes are a pivotal aspect of learning a language. It is equally advantageous for input and output. It also leads to the motivation of the learners, and without motivation, learning is not possible. Rahman (2020) is of the view that English is an important part of any education system, so English language syllabi and methods should be designed to attract students to learning.

Yang and Bao (2023) also supported the idea that teachers' dominance and old-fashioned learning ways are some of the problematic areas for English language learning and that they can play a negative role in learning. Sandagsuren et al. (2022) found that rural area learners need simpler yet attractive ways to learn the English language. Hajar and Manan (2022) expressed that in rural areas, learners are looking for a teacher to dominate the classroom. If the teacher is smart enough to shift them towards autonomy, the classroom might be effective.

The government has worked to upgrade the facilities of rural schools, but not all rural areas have seen the same level of development. Even the most basic infrastructural amenities, like access to appropriate information and communication technologies (ICT) education, are still lacking in many places. Even though the government has given schools access to technological resources, many of them are not operating efficiently. Particularly in rural areas, there are no proper ICT resources. This is due to varied reasons, such as the restricted ability of administration, teachers and students to access the facilities, users' limited knowledge and programmes that do not adequately serve the needs of rural students. Before launching any programme, it's perilous to evaluate the local circumstances and the goals of rural students in order to improve technology-based education in rural areas of Pakistan. In order to conduct this assessment, beneficiaries in rural areas should be surveyed and engaged in a dialogue. The ultimate goal should be to assist students in rural areas.

ESL learning depends significantly on the environment being conducive and supportive. However, in rural areas, various factors hinder students' learning rather than helping them. The rural setting, agricultural lifestyle, lack of education and poverty often result in parents not prioritising their children's education, especially in ESL learning. Many parents show little or no interest in their children's ESL learning due to their own limited education and the challenging circumstances they face to meet their living. The uneducated and rural environment negatively impacts learners, whereas living in an educated community can enhance students' learning efficiency (Positive involvement in these factors can significantly boost learning outcomes. Unfortunately, many parents fail to recognise the importance of English, which is widely regarded as a key to success in the modern era, particularly in professional fields like engineering, medicine, agriculture, zoology and literature (Rahman, 2006).

English proficiency not only aids in accessing modern literature and technology but also opens doors to global communication, as English is the language of international discourse in today's interconnected world. The researchers focused on family factors as they form the foundation for learning; without encouragement and support at home, students' potential remains untapped. The rural upbringing and lack of parental support significantly impede ESL learning among rural students.

### Reflections of Some Apropos Studies

Ma et al. (2023) executed an enquiry to explore computer-assisted learning's worth on the performance of rural students in mathematics. The sample size was huge, with 1840 students from 95 schools participating in the study by the local average treatment effect. It was explored that math performance has a significant connection with computer learning. The local average treatment also suggested that using computer learning for more than 20 minutes per week can be extremely beneficial for learners. Meng et al. (2023) explored the area of games in connection with computer-enhanced language learning (CELL) for EFL lessons in rural ambience. Through a qualitative method, data were collected. The tools used were a questionnaire and interviews for the opinions of the participants. The said sample consisted of students aged from 10 to 12. The teachers and parents were also part of the study to provide their opinions. It was shared that CELL games provided motivation for rural learners to learn English.

It also developed interest. Both teachers and parents authenticated the improvement in the performance of students.

Some local studies on rural areas were also performed, but they were not related to CELL, specifically in the rural areas.

Akram et al. (2020) conducted an investigation looking at the challenges and then giving solutions for improving English in rural places. By using a qualitative approach, 18 instructors (12 women and six men) collected data through observations and interviews inside the classrooms. Later, by analysing the themes, they concluded their findings. They found out that English learning history, background, course length, shortage of resources, overpopulation of the class and lack of competent teachers are the major predicaments in learning English. They suggested having regular English classes with qualified teachers in a completely new and well-developed classroom.

Bhurgri et al. (2020) also looked at the issues of rural area learners in government schools. They had a sample of 60 students from 13 to 18 years old in a rural area belonging to the Sargodha district. A survey helped them gather data about factors that were creating problems in English learning in rural scenarios. They pointed out that, apart from family issues, curriculum, classroom teaching methods and laborious teaching styles are the biggest issues in rural areas. All of these problems can be resolved if the latest method can be introduced in rural areas. The above-mentioned studies explored multiple factors faced by rural area learners, but all of these studies were confined to the presentation of the problems. Rural area students are rigorous in their learning, but they face difficulties in learning the English language. Only memorisation is encouraged, and no modern way of learning is utilised. Hence, there is room for investigating these learners to equip them with modern ways.

These studies provide a gap in conducting research on implementing the latest method, that is, CELL, as there is a need for conducting research on rural area learners for incorporating CELL in the Pakistani context to provide an example for the concerns. This research would strive to explore some potential points of CELL in rural areas. This study will also create an opening for future researchers to explore the latest methods to overcome English language learning issues in Pakistan.

## Theoretical Foundations

Among the various research theories connected with the CELL, a significant one is the Engagement Theory. This theory was developed by O'Brien and Toms (2008) as a theoretical basis to define the engagement of users and technology, encompassing experiences beyond educational contexts. Their work produced a conceptual model applicable to various domains, such as technology-dependent learning. O'Brien and Toms' (2008) theory of engagement in technology is characterised by elements such as challenge, aesthetic attraction, response, innovation, interaction, perceived control, time consciousness, enthusiasm, interest and emotional response. This conceptual model delineates different phases of the engagement process, including the initiation and sustainability of engagement, disengagement and potential reengagement with the system over time. The Engagement Theory, proposed by Kearsley and Schneiderman (1998), serves as a basis for technology-dependent instruction and learning. Its core principle emphasises the importance of meaningful encounters in learning actions by interacting with others and meaningful tasks. While engagement can theoretically occur without technology, Kearsley and Schneiderman argue that technology can enhance engagement in unique ways that may be challenging to achieve otherwise. O'Brien and Toms' (2008) conceptual framework aligns with the Engagement Theory by emphasising independent and realistic involvement with resources or applications, focusing on mental challenges and inspirations. The Engagement Theory emphasises the creation of fruitful collaborative teams working on meaningful projects relevant to real-world contexts, encapsulated in the concepts of relate, create and donate. This framework highlights that learning actions should occur in group settings, be like a project and should have authentic attention outside the classroom. O'Brien and Toms' (2008) framework goes beyond traditional usability concepts in human-computer interactions, focusing on defining an engaged user experience with technology. Through their research, they identify engagement as an experience gained by the user characterised by qualities such as challenge, aesthetic appeal, response, innovation, interaction, perceived control, time consciousness, enthusiasm, attention and emotional response. The framework also outlines an engagement process with the following four potential stages: The point of engagement where it begins, the period of engagement, disengagement and reengagement. This iterative aspect of reengagement allows users to pause interactions and resume later. Each stage is associated with distinct attributes that contribute to the overall engagement experience. To gain a deeper understanding of any theory, it is essential to grasp the foundational principles that underpin that theory. The same applies to the Engagement Theory. These principles can be summarised as follows:

**Relate:** Engaging in learning through collaborative efforts with others.
**Create:** Embracing a project-oriented approach to learning.
**Donate:** Learning with a focus on real-world applications and external relevance (Shahbaznezhad et al., 2021).

These features look to construct realistic situations while demanding learners to utilise their minds to solve problems. They also emphasise making decisions after evaluation. Each goal is connected with the internal motivation.

The practical aspects of this theory are as follows:

1. **Engaged learning through relatability**
   This principle focuses on encouraging students to exchange perspectives with their peers and establish connections with what they contribute and receive. It involves fostering active and meaningful collaboration among students, which can be facilitated through interactive tutorials. Educators should design activities that promote teamwork, communication, planning and social skills among students. In an ideal scenario, students would actively engage with and relate to their peers' approaches to the topic and derive insights from them (Bitrián et al., 2021). Another crucial aspect of learning through relatability is the ability to defend ideas. In classrooms where there is active discussion among students, various ideas are often presented. The opportunity to comprehend these concepts, question areas of uncertainty and defend their own ideas can stimulate intrinsic motivation for learning, which is essential (Rapp et al., 2021).

2. **Fosters creativity in students**

This principle emphasises adopting a project-based approach to learning that encourages creativity and purposefulness. Educators should design activities that allow students to engage in creative projects where they define concepts in their own terms, organise information and create something that reflects their understanding. Through such projects, students can develop a sense of ownership and responsibility for their learning, leading to intrinsic motivation.

3. **Encouraging engaged learning through contribution**

While the first two principles emphasised an internal focus on students themselves, this principle emphasised an external or authentic focus. It involves engaging in activities that benefit a third party, such as a customer or an external organisation. Educators can guide students to undertake projects that address the needs of external entities like student groups, museums, government agencies, schools or local organisations. These projects have a practical aspect as they focus on meeting the needs of others, requiring students to consider perspectives outside their own. This approach fosters motivation among students, enhances their learning and prepares them for future roles in their respective fields (Chaves & Gerosa, 2021). Using technology to facilitate student collaboration involves students working together with peers and educators to express, question and defend ideas. This collaborative process extends beyond the classroom and requires a variety of activities both in and out of class. Communication systems, such as email, chat groups and video conferencing tools, play a crucial role in enabling students to exchange ideas effectively. Another essential aspect is providing ways for students to express ideas through tactile examples. Technologies like design and 3D printing allow students to create physical models and figures that enhance the expression and understanding of ideas. Moreover, technology enables students to contribute to external needs by providing access to resources, organisations and knowledge that would otherwise be inaccessible. The internet serves as a valuable connectivity tool, allowing students to understand and cater to the requirements of third parties. Virtual solutions, such as virtual wireframe models, bridge the gap for customers who require physical objects or field visits, enabling students to meet the needs of distant entities effectively.

## Previous Researches

Wang (2024) executed a study to look at the engagement of students as a pivotal predictor of academic performance in second-language classrooms. Focusing on the Engagement Theory, this research collected data from various dimensions, like a preliminary survey, discussions (audio) and interviews, which were retrospective. The outcomes shared some significant aspects, including that the engagement of learners through computer-based activities leads to task completion perfectly. The study also shared that the learners' engagement not only promoted their language ability but also developed their cognitive aspect of learning.

Gray and DiLoreto (2016) conducted research that showed the relationship between the interaction of learners, their engagement and the presence of the instructor as well. Their research also reflected the satisfaction of the students. They concluded that online teaching and learning and using technology tools enhance students' engagement. Moreover, they also reflected that technology gadgets add variety to the stream of learning and thus increase engagement amongst students. This uplifted their performance.

Nguyen et al. (2017) did research on finding the value of computer-constructed evaluations regarding their affordability. According to Engagement Theory, the real aspect was to know about the configuration of the culture centered aapproach (CCA), modules and the effect of evaluation design on the engagement of students. The analysis was performed using a combination of visualisation and correlation analysis. The outcomes indicated that the value of CCA design has become highly significant and valuable for learners. They also reflected that the pass ratio was related to the learners' activities, which was due to their engagement with computers.

Shernoff et al. (2003) performed one of the early investigations validating the importance of Engagement Theory. Through a longitudinal sampling of 526 learners across the USA, they investigated how learners were engaged in learning by computers. The experiment revealed that the learners were quite involved in group and individual work as compared to listening to lectures or learning. This suggests that computer mediation increases the involvement of learners and provides autonomy for them.

### Objectives of the Research

The objectives of the research are as follows:

- To apply CELL in rural classrooms in Pakistan.
- To see if there is any positive impact of CELL on rural learners.

### Research Question

- What influence does CELL have on rural English learners?

### Methodology

Any study needs a specific research design relevant to its approach and process to achieve accurate results (Ali et al., 2023). This study uses a quantitative method for extracting results, which is most relevant to inquire about any phenomenon. This study was done in a rural setting, and five villages were part of it. From each village, 20 learners were included in the study. These villages were in Kasur district, Punjab, Pakistan. All these villages had one public school where the study was conducted.

### Steps of the Research

The research was constructed using the following steps:

At first, 20 students were taken from each public school in each of the five villages. In this way, the total number of the students was 100. In the next step, an initial test was done to explore their existing knowledge and performance so that teachers could get an idea of the learner's knowledge and performance. Viewing the results, these 20 students were then assigned equally (ten each) to two different groups in such a way that mixed-ability students were sent to each group, which stopped unconscious bias in the sample. In the next step, teaching sessions were conducted with the two groups for a month. Both groups were taught their already-prescribed syllabus from the Government of the Punjab School Education Department, Pakistan. The teacher was the same for both groups.

To make the research more valid, some important variables were also considered. The time of the class, gender of the students, age of the students, their level of English and the teaching duration for both groups were all constant.

Class timing was 45 minutes in the morning for both groups; students were male, and their age range was from 13 to 14 years. Their level of English was already checked by the initial test. The setting and class were also the same for both. The duration of the process of the experiment was 1 month.

The only intervention came from the independent variable, which was a book (traditional way) for the controlled-group students and CELL for the experimental-group learners.

## Results

The results of experimental and controlled groups' pre-testing procedures by independent-sample $t$-testing method are given in Table 7.1.

The homogenous values assumed showed a variance of $F$: .391, which is less than .05. This value shares that the pre-test was invariant in the two groups. Then, the values of the initial test show that a marginal difference was there in both groups' performance; that is, the MN of the EXP group was 8.76 and the CNT group was 8.72, whereas $t$ was −1.95, which is greater than .01. This value authenticated that EXP group's value (MN) was higher than CNT group's value.

**Table 7.1**  Comparison of Performance of EXP and CNT in Pre-testing

| VARIABLE | EXP (NO = 100) | | CNT (NO = 100) | | | | | 95% CI | | CH |
|---|---|---|---|---|---|---|---|---|---|---|
| | MN | SN | M | SN | FV | t (118) | P | LLT | ULT | d |
| Pre-test | 8.76 | 0.92 | 8.72 | 0.91. | .391 | −1.95 | .006 | −0.21 | −0.18 | 0.42 |

*Abbreviations:*   EXP: experiment group; CNT: controlled group; MN: mean; SN: standard deviation; FV: variance of frequency; CH: Cohen; CI: confidence interval; LLT: lower limit; ULT: upper limit.

**Table 7.2** Comparison of Performance of EXP and CNT in Post-Testing

| VARIABLE | EXPERIMENTAL GROUP (N = 60) | | CONTROL GROUP (N = 60) | | | | | 95% CI | | CH |
|---|---|---|---|---|---|---|---|---|---|---|
| | MN | SN | MN | SN | FV | t (118) | P | LLT | ULT | D |
| Post-test | 17.21 | 2.13 | 10.97 | 1.60 | .045 | −24.94 | .000 | −4.97 | −3.85 | 3.88 |

Going on, the variance in the magnitude was 0.42, which is represented by CH (Cohen's). This value indicates that the size of the effect comes under the medium range of difference in the magnitude

Results of experimental and controlled groups' post-testing procedures by the independent-sample $t$-testing method are given in Table 7.2

The homogentisic values assumed showed a variance of $F$: .045, which is less than .05. This value shares that the post-test was invariant in the two groups. Then, the values of the initial test show that a marginal difference was there in both groups' performance; that is, the mean (MN) of the EXP group was 17.21 and the CNT group was 10.97, whereas $t$ was −24.94, which was greater than .01. This value authenticated that EXP group's (MN) was remarkably higher than CNT group's value. Going on, the variance in the magnitude was 0.45, which is represented by CH (Cohen's). This value indicates that the size of the effect comes in a large range of differences in magnitude.

Results of controlled groups' pre-post-testing procedures by paired-sample $t$-testing method are given in Table 7.3.

The values refer to notable changes that can be observed in the values of pre- and post-testing procedures of the CNT group. The $t$ value is −24.34, which is less than .001. This indicates that the MN score of the post/final test procedure (10.97) was better than the pre-testing procedure (8.72). Likewise, a change can be observed in the SN values too. The size of the effect is 3.99, and it refers to the margin difference in the magnitude.

**Table 7.3** Comparison of Performance of CNT in Pre- and Post-Testing Procedure

| VARIABLE | PRE-TEST | | POST-TEST | | | | 95% CI | | |
|---|---|---|---|---|---|---|---|---|---|
| | M | SD | M | SD | t (149) | P | LL | UL | CH |
| Control Group | 8.72 | 0.91 | 10.97 | 1.60 | −24.34 | .000 | −3.11 | −1.9 | 3.99 |

**Table 7.4**   Comparison of Performance of EXP in Pre- and Post-Testing Procedure

| VARIABLE | PRE-TEST | | POST-TEST | | | | 95% CI | | |
|---|---|---|---|---|---|---|---|---|---|
| | M | SD | M | SD | t (149) | P | LL | UL | CH |
| Experimental Group | 8.76 | 0.92 | 17.21 | 2.13 | -63.41 | .000 | −6.79 | −5.93 | 5.88 |

Results of experimental groups' pre-post-testing procedures by paired-sample *t*-testing method are given in Table 7.4.

The values refer to notable changes that can be observed in the values of pre- and post-testing procedures of the EXP group. The *t* value is −63.41, which is less than .001. This indicates that the MN score of the post-testing procedure (17.21) was better than the pre-testing procedure (8.76). Likewise, a change can be observed in the SN values too. The size of the effect represented by CH (Cohen's) is 5.88, and it refers to the large difference in the magnitude.

### Findings

Some interesting findings are extracted from the results of this study. The SPSS analysis gives a reflection of the tables before and after the experimentation. Seeing the bar chart at the initial test, the performance of both groups was somewhat equal. This proves that, using the traditional method, learners were somehow performing on the same scale. This conclusion was extracted by applying an independent-sample *t*-testing procedure. The paired-sample *t*-testing method also showed the performance comparison of both groups at the post-test, which indicated that the values in the post-test tables of both groups are notably different. The performance of the participants in the traditional group improved, but not significantly. On the other hand, the experimentation group's performance increased remarkably, thus showing the impact of the experimentation. The validity and reliability can be observed by the values of Cronbach alpha. To sum up, the effect of CELL as a modern method has been proven statistically. It is shared that both groups have vivid differences in their performances. Thus, the experiment proves the effectiveness of CELL.

## Discussion

CELL has augmented the value of English language teaching. The direct interaction between learners and teachers is mediated by the CELL. It has emerged as an alternative to already-existing ways of teaching and learning. This study was designed to see if CELL is efficient in rural areas amongst English language learners. The observations and findings suggest that CELL is a meaningful method for creating a positive impact on learning. The findings of this study are connected to earlier studies like Park and Son (2022), who shared that CELL is pivotal in the development of learning. It also helps to uplift the motivation and proficiency of the language of the learner (Rafiee & Abbasian-Naghneh, 2021).

Son (2018) is of the opinion that English lessons can be frustrating due to their traditional ways, so CELL can be a prolific replacement for creating interest in learning. The intervention in this study by CELL proves its value. The high scores of the experimental groups are proof that they enjoyed learning through CELL.

In other words, CELL had a positive impact on learners' vocabulary learning. Thus, it validates that the outcomes penned down here shared that the use of CELL-supported software stimulates positive emotions to learn better. The conclusions are in a similar vein to the results of Rahimi and Allahyari (2019), who investigated whether vocabulary can be developed by CELL. They found that those who used this software had better improvement in their vocabulary knowledge than those who did not use it. The above finding is also supported by the finding of Kaur et al. (2023), who indicated that the technology-driven groups are more motivated and take a deep interest in learning (Gray et al., 2010). This study also advocated the usefulness of CELL as a learning technique in classrooms where English learning becomes a problem due to various factors (Weisset al., 2019). It can also be observed that, if applied appropriately, these tools can increase engagement among students and increase their mental ability. This is also advocated by Stockwell and Reinders (2019), who believed that learners who are engrossed in collective activities are indulged in mutual communication. They are encouraged to share knowledge, reporting a higher level of achievement, which can increase their fervour than other learners. Some aspects of CELL, like YouTube and other video software, permit content distribution in contrast with documents or textbooks. Classically, countryside institutes feature advanced stages of scholars learning English who might favour the use of pictorial learning, in addition to captions, for developing their understanding (Yentes & Gaskill, 2015). Teachers in Pakistan are not accustomed to using CELL. This is evidently shown in the findings here. These findings are also connected to the earlier exploration which showed that institutes that are present in the countryside rarely use computers in their academics. Contrariwise, those rural institutes which exhibit better learning utilise computers in their academics. Findings here showed that countryside institutes exploited technology and found it an important tool. However, they also found some hindrances to its integration. Eppley (2021) said that it is mandatory for teachers to get training for utilising different tools for in-class assignments and activities. Moreover, this research also shared that CELL's effect can increase motivation, attentiveness and collaboration (Jones & Dexter, 2018).

From the perspective of Engagement Theory, this research continues along the line of Engagement Theory. The results of this investigation proclaim that learners' academic achievement is due to their engagement in learning. This is the core principle of the Engagement Theory, which portrays that meaningful connections for learning are fruitful for producing excellence in learning.

Also, the learners relate their knowledge through collaboration. This can help them understand the concept of the subject. Moreover, the discussion amongst the learners can also contribute to the creation of new knowledge. This conception is also supported by Shahbaznezhad et al. (2021), who said that for knowledge creation and sharing, learners must converse and discuss with each other. Rapp et al. (2021) shared that for comprehending the new concepts and questioning the uncertain areas, mutual communication is very important. Then, a significant feature of this research. It motivates engagement through conversational contributions (Chaves & Gerosa, 2021). Email, video chats, Zoom groups and WhatsApp calls are magnificent examples of mutual communication (Ali et al., 2023). Going ahead, the feature of showing ideas through tactile examples is another aspect of this theory, which is vivid in his research as well. The use of CELL enabled students to learn varied conceptual aspects through a physical model, which increased their comprehension of ideas. Overall, this study ties knots with Wang (2024), who shared that the learners' engagement is a significant sign that can predict the better performance of learners. Finally, Nguyen et al. (2017) also said that learning is boosted when learners are strung together.

## Conclusion

In this study, a compelling substitute has been observed in the form of CELL for educating students. It can be a good alternative to already established learning methods. Presented through the results and discussion, a conclusive element can be shared: CELL has been the perfect learning tool for students. The lacuna amongst students and teachers in English learning ambiences is perfectly bridged by CELL in this experiment. CELL has shown its worth as a useful supportive tool to assist teachers and students. The rural area students were not exposed to the technology at such a level, but they felt positive and participated vigorously. The conclusive elements successfully presented in the result section display the value of CELL in rural classrooms. In total, students felt enthusiasm, confidence and interest while learning by CELL. The values from the results proved that CELL has been an interesting way to increase the performance of the students, and now it is to be decided by the concerned authorities and the implementors whether to benefit from this technology or not.

## Recommendations

- The infrastructure of rural classrooms should be changed.
- Context-related syllabi should be introduced in rural areas, promoting technology use.
- A comprehensive understanding of CELL should be given to the concerns.
- Pilot projects of CELL under experts should be initiated.
- The teachers involved in the pilot projects must be trained to use CELL.

- District education officers and principals should encourage the use of CELL.
- Students must be made aware of CELL through workshops and discussions.
- Incentives should be introduced for administration and instructors who initiate CELL.
- Smooth connections to the Internet and WI-FI should be given priority.

# 8

# THE APPLICATION OF SMARTBOARDS IN ESP CLASSROOMS

## Introduction and Background

Amongst languages, English inveterate strongly in various fields. The multi-directional opportunities offered by English have opened various English genres for learners. Now, English has gone beyond the borders of classrooms to the utilisation of English for particular needs and purposes. From here, the term English for specific purposes has arisen. Some further divisions of ESP are also there like ESP (science, arts, doctors, engineers, hotel management, etc.). This classification was done thirty years ago (Hutchinson & Waters, 1987). Dabong (2019) found that ESP is pertinent to some specific disciplines and that it is designed for dealing with mostly adult students. Further, it is focused on its goal and is time-restricted. As technology is creating a strong impact on current life, in pedagogy, the experts are keen to introduce unheard and new ways to catch the attention of the students towards learning. Ratheeswai (2018) is of the view that technology is perfectly useful in educational domains. In some of the in-class technologies for pedagogical purposes, it has been observed that smartboards have caught the interest of educators (Tefo & Goosen, 2024). A smartboard, or interactive board, is a tool utilised mainly for educational activities. Apart from that, it is used in offices for conferencing as well. It has a touch-screen surface, which helps with interacting with and presenting digital material like documents, videos, and images. Earlier smartboards were connected to computers, but the latest ones have built-in computers for performing the functions. Being an electric device, it works with either a specific pen or a finger. It also permits it to present, share, and annotate any digital material for its users and audience. Smartboard combines all the earlier

DOI: 10.1201/9781003450733-8

instructional methods like video, TV, blackboard, whiteboard, and computer as well. Moreover, various apps can be opened for the benefit of students. Therefore, it gives multiple chances to the English as a second language/English as a foreign language and English as a special language (ESL/EFL and ESP) instructors to initiate stimulating and sensational ways contrary to existing methods. (Eynel & Koc, 2023).

Smartboards hold significant value in English language learning as well. They energise the learning procedures in any English-language class.

This is one of the reasons for their popularity in worldwide classrooms. Some crucial advantages of smartboards are that they:

- **Increase in learning**
  By providing interactive learning opportunities, smartboards permit the inclusion of some multimedia features that make lessons interactive and interesting. This creates motivation and develops a diverse style of learning.

- **Personalised Pedagogy**
  Smartboards enable resource persons to personalise the teaching according to their desires and requirements. Due to the variation in features ranging from video, images, audio and even digital whiteboards, Smartboards are best for self-preferred styles.

- **Environment friendly**
  The modern world is conscious of taking atmospheric-friendly steps. In this regard, smartboards are the best solution, as they eliminate the requirement for paper and chalk. Secondly, they reduce waste and promote sustainability. As teachers can use and reuse their lessons and can save them anytime, smartboards play an active role in building a green environment.

- **Learning in collaboration**
  Smartboards promote collaborative learning by enabling students to engage in interactive activities, share ideas, work on projects together, and present their work to the class. This fosters a teamwork and community approach among students, encouraging active learning and giving them autonomy for taking ownership.

- **Enhanced learning results**
  Utilizing smartboards provides an interactive and captivating approach to learning, potentially resulting in enhanced retention and superior learning outcomes among students. With smartboards, educators can develop immersive and dynamic lessons tailored to various learning preferences, thereby enhancing accessibility and inclusivity in the learning process.

- **Instant feedback**
  Smartboards offer educators immediate feedback regarding student progress. Through interactive features, teachers can evaluate comprehension levels, pinpoint challenging areas and adapt teaching strategies accordingly. This makes smartboards an invaluable resource for formative assessment purposes.

Some recent literature reflects that the use of smartboards is motivating and striking (Ali et al., 2023). Another study by Jammeh et al. (2023) stated that smartboards impact learners in a positive way and uplift their skills and knowledge. Commenting further on the benefits of smartboards, Herawati et al. (2023) showed that students can be engaged effectively while using smartboards.

Smartboards have infused positivity in ESP classrooms as well. A major element in this regard is engaging the students by attracting them with various activities and methods and asking questions. It creates a social learning hub. Dimitriadou and Lanitis (2023) found that for the development and construction of knowledge and the involvement of learners, smartboards are significantly important. Siregar and Sukmawarti (2022) advocated the value of the smartboard because it increases the participation of students. The digital and technological resources do not allow isolation in learning. Frith (2023) shared that smartboards increase learner and teacher interaction. Further, the addition of multiple software programmes encourages involvement and makes learning easy. Yalman and Basaran (2021) shared that smartboards promote oral activities better than conventional classrooms. Further, it also provided an advantage to the teachers as well. It works as a conjunctive element between the teacher and students. Also, the instructors can utilise various resources without wasting time. The touch-screen user interface is also there for the teacher to write digitally while following the traditional way. In this way, even the orthodox instructors feel relaxed and confident while using the smart board (Petchamé et al., 2023). Another thing is the motivation of learners. It is said that in English language learning, motivation is essential. As previously adopted methods have failed to motivate learners, smartboards can be a good alternative (Bhasin & Lanka, 2022). Research by Ojo et al. (2022) *shared that a smartboard is an* environment with tools that give an additive advantage to learning. Rizk and Hillier (2022) viewed collaboration as a major element of smartboard learning. Moreover, learning flexibility, variety and connectivity are the major positives of a smartboard.

Fawaz (2022) conducted a study on the effect of the smartboard on young schoolchildren in primary school. Through a quasi-experimental design, the study was performed. The intervention and impact of the smart board were examined by pre- and post-tests. The pretest was taken by all through conventional tests, and then the experiment group students learned by smartboard. In the end, a post-test revealed the better performance of the experiment group students. Also, a questionnaire was structured to look at the motivation level of students. The outcomes showed that experimenters were motivated and energetic when they were exposed to smart board classrooms.

Coronel (2023) explored the value of smartboards for teaching. This was a post-pandemic study where the teachers were given training to use smartboards for their learning. These four teachers underwent eight weeks of training and learned a lot of techniques and ways to use smart boards. It was scripted by them that a smart board is an important tool used to teach with innovation and ease. They also shared that the large screen option., mirroring and other features give them a lot of space to teach significantly.

Mun et al. (2019) did an exploration to identify the effectiveness of learning through a smart board. This study was done in the mathematics context, where 30 students were chosen. All of them were five years old. The learners were chosen by purposive sampling. The study used a mixed-methods approach. The results showed that the students performed well as compared to their earlier performance, which was shared through a descriptive result. Further, the theme analysis of the opinion showed that the learners felt happy, energetic and motivated while learning on the smartboard.

Smartboard use in many countries is multipurpose, but in Pakistan, it has not been used, particularly in ESP settings. Considering the acceptance of technology in pedagogy, this research will explore the utility of smartboards for ESP learners. This will be the first study of its nature in the local vicinity, and it will open up many new paths for future investigators interested in exploring more pedagogical tools.

## Past Researchers on Smartboard

Huseynova (2023) had a study on the exploration for discussing the strategies, benefits and results of applying smartboards in English language learning situations. They found out that there are numerous advantages to smartboards, like the easy revival of previous materials and lectures. It also has interactivity for the learners, and it supports a collaborative ambiance for learning. It permits instructors to develop vocabulary and boosts the confidence of the participants.

Hussein et al. (2022) inspected the vitality of smartboards for academic situations. To achieve the results, they developed 28 questions and shared them with forty teachers in a purposive sampling way. Twenty of them were from the chemistry and biology departments, and twenty of them were from the Arabic and history departments. This variety gave a wider horizon to the study. The results mirrored multiple benefits of the smartboard to the teachers. However, they also showed problems and structural issues with implementing smartboards in teaching affairs. It was concluded that a smartboard boosts learning affairs while giving support through a variety of digital features to its users.

## Framework

Activity theory, called as AT, is a comprehensive framework rooted in Soviet psychological theories developed by scholars like Sergei Rubinstein and promoted by Alexei Leont'ev. It emerged as a foremost mental approach and has been extensively applied in various fields such as academics, work, social psychology, etc (Hashim & Jones, 2007). AT is a widely recognised framework within organisational practice-based approaches. It focuses on the concept of "activity". According to this theory, human behaviour is intricately linked to mutually systematised actions (Marwan & Sweeney, 2019).

AT origins are multifaceted, leading to diverse and interconnected developmental paths. A pivotal starting point is linked to the Moscow Institute of Psychology, notably the trio of Vygotsky, Leont'ev and Luria (Leontiev, 1978; Vygotsky & Luria, 1994). A key strength of AT is its ability to linkup single subjects and social veracities by reviewing both interventional activities. The analysis unit in AT is the orientation of an object that is dipped in the culturally connected human activity, known as the activity structure (Maidansky, 2021). This structure comprises elements like objective/object, the subject, tools and signs, rules, community, and management of labour. Motivation in AT is generated through contradictions and tensions within these elements of the system (Tlili et al., 2022). Ren and Zhu (2023) noted that interest in AT develops from its conscious effort to avoid the pitfalls of separating thought from action and individuals from collectivities, as often seen in Western intellectual tradition. Vygotsky, as in Yamagata-Lynch and Yamagata-Lync (2010), emphasised the interconnectedness of internal and external activities, highlighting the social origins of cognition, learning and development. This perspective underscores the role of signs and cultural artifacts in mediating human action, as outlined in Vygotsky's model and its reformulation by Foot (2001). Engestrom (1987) further advanced AT by emphasising collective activity, drawing from Leontyev's ideas. Engestrom's formulation of activity includes subjects acting on objects through mediating tools within a pertinent community, complete with norms and labor division. While Leontyev (1977), as in Leontiev (2006), highlighted the importance of motives driving activities, Engestrom (2001) expanded on this by introducing the concept of a community and its regulations influencing interactions within an activity. AT is a descriptive framework and theory rather than a predictive one, focusing on observing human actions as an organised, systematic and social phenomenon. It considers entire work or activity systems, including teams and organisations, rather than focusing solely on individual actors or users (Nazari & Karimpour, 2022). AT views factors such as the environment, the individual's history, cultural influences, the role of artifacts, motivations and the complexity of real-life activities.

The concept of activity comprises three key components:

- subjects,
- objects,
- and mediating tools.

These tools can be both material and conceptual, produced through other activities, and used across various contexts. Wartofsky (1973) contributed to this understanding by highlighting humans' unique ability to create and use tools, which are integral to human activity.

The theory looked at what participants do within a community contextually, bridging the gap between individual actions and collective practices. Leontyev (2006) as in Blunden (2021) looked at the differentiation between activity, actions, and operations underscores the interconnectedness of human needs, motives, and goal-directed actions within activities. This linkage is crucial for understanding complex organisational phenomena involving multiple teams and diverse actions. Cultural-Historical Activity Theory, a variant of AT, has been particularly useful for studying groups that primarily interact virtually, such as those communicating through electronic and printed texts. It has also been used in other genres, like writing studies, while looking at how the communication can share the relationships, processes of work and the societal information (Lee et al., 2022).

Researchers have applied AT to various domains, including software development, to better understand collaboration, human interaction and problem-solving processes. The framework's ability to capture the complexity, contextuality and contested nature of activities makes it a valuable tool for analysing and improving organisational practices. (Figure 8.1)

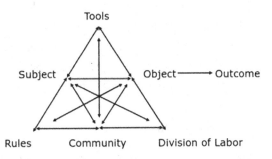

**Figure 8.1**   Activity theory model. (Roschelle, 1998)

Nardi (1995), a prominent AT theorist, emphasises that AT focuses on comprehending daily practices in the actual world, making distinctions between "applied" and "pure" science unnecessary. AT aims to comprehend the union of awareness and action.

AT serves as a valuable framework in qualitative research methodologies like ethnography and case studies. It offers a method for comprehending and analysing phenomena, identifying designs, drawing inferences across communications and explaining the phenomena. In AT, an action is a meaningful connection between a subject and an object facilitated by the utilisation of tools. These tools encompass a wide range, including physical and digital gadgets and even physical places used for meetings (Cong-Lem, 2022). AT admits the worth of mental processes while using tools. Further, it also supports the change that occurs as a result of these interactions with technology tools

While the primary objective of AT is to comprehend an individual's mental abilities, it discards the notion of isolated persons as an inadequate unit for the analysis. Instead, it emphasises the analysis of technical and cultural aspects inherent in human activities within socio-technical systems. AT provides valuable insights into how social artifacts and organisational structures influence human interactions within complex socio-technical environments (Zhang et al., 2024). It offers a descriptive tool rather than a predictive theory, aiming to understand the unity of consciousness and activity. According to Nardi, AT emphasises the role of mediation in shaping human experiences through tools and sign systems. Consciousness, as per AT, encompasses various mental operations such as consideration, intent, memory, speech, and reasoning all influenced by social interactions and exploitation of tools (Gogus, 2023).

Furthermore, in the field of information and communications technology (ICT) and development, AT has guided the expansion of IT systems (Tsai et al., 2020). Recent work has also delved into using social media interfaces to mediate conflicts and explore identity maintenance in various contexts, showcasing the relevance and applicability of AT in contemporary research areas (Jiang & Yu, 2022).

## Past Research on the Activity Theory

Dai et al., (2022) executed an investigation of the efficacy of ICT-supported teaching methods through the eyes of AT, looking at the satisfaction and interaction of engineering discipline learners. The experiment suggested that AT has practical validity as the ICT-based ways increase learners' interaction in the experiment group. Moreover, in contrast with orthodox-style learners, they were 83.7% more satisfied with the ICT-based learning method. Also, 70.3% of learners shared this as their favourite way of learning. Hajimaghsoodi and Maftoon (2020) explored the students' achievement in second language writing while using computer technology. Using AT as their edifice, the learners were put into an experiment. A total of 67 learners were part of the study. Using a mixed-methods approach, data were collected, which consisted of a written pre-and post-test, two questionnaires, and an interview that was semi-structured. This comprehensive study gave some vital results, which stated that learners' achievement got better in computer-based language learning. They shared that AT provided a reference point for learners as a purposeful interaction between a subject and an object was made. This means learners connected to computers in terms of writing skills have learned magnificently.

Li et al. (2022), in their research, applied AT to describe and analyse a project that was out of school. The learners were eight Chinese students who were engaged in an online game that was massively multiplayer for English language learning. The data collection was from questionnaires, various journals from games, recordings of games and interviews as well. Moreover, theme analysis was also performed to look at the themes present in it. The evidence collected from this research reported that learners were found to be autonomous. They also gained vocabulary and confidence in their oral and written fluency. It also showed that digital games can be advantageous for learning. All these studies created vivid evidence that smartboards are found to be diversely impactful and effective. Viewing these studies also showed a research space where there is no notable study on smartboards in indigenous settings. Therefore, the satisfaction calls for a study to view the impact of Smartboard in indigenous scenarios. Therefore, this study will focus on viewing the smartboard's impact on local ambiance.

## Methods of Research

For investigating the outcomes from the application of smartboards, there was a need for some pertinent methodology. To serve this, interpretive research was adopted. Pervin and Mokhtar (2023) directed that interpretive research looks for an understanding of any social phenomena and human attitude or behaviour in which any audience is involved.

Being a descriptive exploration, the interpretive method was found to be appropriate for the assessment of the outcomes.

## Population

Research was conducted on the population of Pakistan. All the ESP students who were studying the ESP course were the specific population chosen for the investigation.

## Sample

The sample for this research was taken from the chosen population. At first, Multan was chosen as a sample. Population-wise, Multan is the biggest city in South Punjab, Pakistan. The city was picked up by a convenient method of sampling. In Multan, a culinary institute was preferred by the pick-and-choose process.

Hundred students who were taking an ESP course named English for Culinary Management from these universities were picked. So, twenty students were part of the study at one university. All these students were then divided into groups of two. One was named control, and the other was experimental.

## Objectives

- To investigate the application of Smartboard in pedagogical settings
- To see if there is any positive effect of the smartboard on ESP students

## Questions for Research

- What impact does Smartboard have on ESP students in the Pakistani context?

## Research Process

In the next step, an initial test was done to explore their existing knowledge and performance. In this way, teachers get an idea of the knowledge and performance of the participants. Viewing the results, mixed-ability students were sent to each group, which stopped unconscious bias in the sample. In the next step, teaching sessions were conducted with the two groups for a month. Both groups were taught their already prescribed syllabus by the Punjab Government in Pakistan. The teacher was the same for both groups.

To make the research more valid, some important variables were also considered. The time of the class, the age of the students, their level of English, and the teaching duration for both groups were all constants for both groups.

Class timing was 45 minutes in the morning for both groups; students ages ranged from 13 to 14 years, and their level of English was already checked by the initial test. The setting and classroom were also the same for both groups. The duration of the experiment was one month.

The only intervention came from the independent variable, which was book (traditional way) for the controlled-group students and CELL for the experimental-group learners.

### Analysis of the Dataset

*Standard deviation: SN*
*Variance of Frequency: FV*
*Cohen: CH*
CIN = Confidence Interval,
*LLT=* Lower Limit,
*ULT* = Upper Limit.

*Comparison of Performance CNT and EXP in Pretesting,*
*Paired Sample T-test*

In Figure 8.2, various values are interpreted in the form of graphs. Looking at the mean-value in the initial tests, the two group scores were almost similar (8.57 for CNTRL and 8.58 for EXPT). Also, there is equality amongst both clusters in standard deviation denoted by SN and T values as well. This vividly advocates that both groups belong to similar abilities, and before any intervention of independent variable, they performed identically.

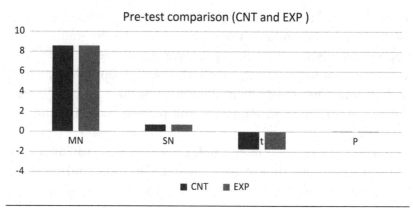

**Figure 8.2** Pre_post test comparison.

*Comparison of Performance of EXP and CNT in Post Testing, Paired Sample T-test*

This chart describes the values of both clusters after the experiment process. The values are shown through bar chart. The mean difference amongst groups has a significant difference (9.11 for Control and 16.12 for experiment) clusters. It presents that after intervention of the independent variable the scores of experiment cluster learners were almost doubled. The standard deviation values for both were 1.62 for the control and 2.17 for experiment group. Overall, the post-test results authenticate the effectiveness of the tool applied as an experiment. (Figure 8.3)

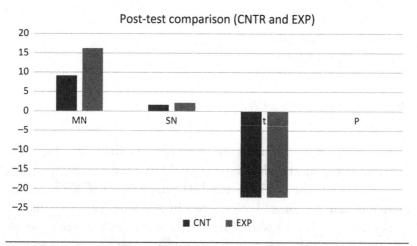

**Figure 8.3** Pre and post test comparison.

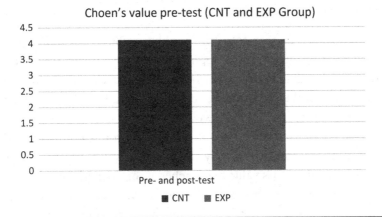

**Figure 8.4**   Cohen's value pre test of controlled and experiment group.

Figure 8.4 is about Cohen's value, which mirrors the test in terms of its reliability and validity. The magnitude of differences in the experimental and the control group between pre-test and post-test assessments was measured at 4.11, indicating a medium effect size according to Cohen's d value (Cohen, 1992).

This chart illustrates Cohen's value, reflecting the test's validity and reliability. The difference in magnitude between the pre-test and post-test assessments for both the experimental and control groups was calculated at 6.16, indicating a moderate effect size as per Cohen's d value (Cohen, 1992). (Figure 8.5)

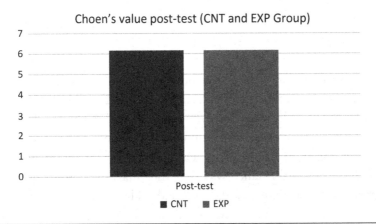

**Figure 8.5**   Cohen's value post test of controlled and experiment group.

Findings and Discussion

The findings can be seen from the bar charts above. An independent sample *t*-testing method was applied for the analysis of the dataset. Initial test data has been shown in the first bar chart, which stated no difference in the performance of both groups. Control and experiment were almost at the same level.

The second bar chart, however, is different from the first one. The post-test results are distinctively different between the two groups. The experiment group's value has reached a considerable point of 18.1, whereas the value for the control group is 9.8. This vivid variation in the performance of the pos-test results of the experiment group is a reflection of the intervention of the smartboard. Therefore, statistically, it is proven through the sample that smartboards have an influence on learners. Also, the reliability of the test was examined through Cronbach's alpha. The values in the above table show that both pre-and post-tests of both control and experiment cluster groups were reliable.

Moving on to the discussion, there are some important elements of the smartboard that have impacted the experiment learners and were the cause of their better performance. These elements were also shown by various researchers in their investigations.

These aspects are

- Oral activities
- Motivation
- Collaboration
- Participation
- Fun-learning

Coronel (2023) says that smartboards are key elements in promoting oral activities among students. This was also found in this experiment, where the learners were involved in oral activities, through which their speaking was improved. Further, the smartboard increases the motivation of the learners stated that one factor that created better performance was that the smartboard motivated the learners profusely. Elma et al., (2024) also claimed that smartboards are important in elevating the motivation of learners. Uninteresting was making learners disinterested in learning. The inclusion of a smartboard gave them enthusiasm and motivation to be agile and active. In this way, the results are connected to this research Fawaz (2022) viewed smartboards as the best tools to boost the motivation of ESL learners. Modern classrooms are interactive and promote collaboration. The results particularised that kids favour to connect with the smartboard as it was attractive and engaging for them. Ratheeswai (2018) viewed collaboration as a key aspect of improving learning through smartboards. So, using a smartboard can be a perfect substitution for current teaching methods by giving multiple options to its users. This is validated by this investigation as well, in which the students were collaborating and interacting in a motivated environment. This follows the steps of Ojo et al. (2022) research, which stated that smartboard activities encourage collaboration. Then, participation here refers to individual participation and group participation. In this study, the teacher planned activities that required learners to participate. Further, the activities demanded learners' participation, and they were student-focused. Therefore, comparing with the already-running teaching method, the learners were involved and participated in the activities. Eynel and Koc (2023) also concluded that smartboard activities attract learners to participate in learning. On this aspect, this research shares commonality with Tefo and Goosen (2024), who verdict that smartboards link individuals and groups to participate actively. Finally, a chief aspect of Smartboard is fun learning. Usual classrooms in local settings are text-book-based, where a whiteboard with markers is used. The students are only watching their teacher write and memorise. On the other hand, smartboards have many apps that are fun-learning, improve students' confidence, and also encourage their involvement. Dimitriadou and Lanitis (2023) say that technology converts difficult learning ways to easy ones. Therefore, through Padlet, Quizzes, Kahoot and other apps, learners are entertained and also learn. This aspect was also found in this exploration, where the teachers had the opportunity to use different fun-loving activities, which created a relaxing yet comfortable and enjoyable environment. Overall, the statistical findings and discussion join with the research of Huseynova (2023) and Hussein et al. (2022), who found out the worth of using smartboards and shared that smartboards are indeed a beneficial tool for English learning.

Looking at the results from ATs perspective. This research has the characteristics shared by AT. In theory, activity means the meaningful connection between subject and object, which is supported by the utilisation of tools. Tools can include digital and physical tools (Cong-Lem, 2022). In this exploration, it is evident that the smartboard acts as a meaningful tool for developing connections between learners and the ESP course. Moreover, another aspect of AT is that it motivates learners to learn by filling the gap between individual subjects and social realities (Maidansky, 2021). This feature is also present in this research, where the gap was filled by the subject, which was English, and the social reality that English has always been a problematic area in Pakistan. Therefore, by performing the activity, the connection was developed for better learning paths. Tlili et al. (2022) looked at elements or objects like tools, rules, signs and labor division. According to them, the motivation in this theory is constructed by the presence of these elements. This is also vivid in this research, where the learning of the subject was directly proportional to the tool, i.e., the smartboard. The pressure of learning English was less when the learners learned through the smartboard, or, in other words, the motivation they got after learning from the smart board helped to overcome the learning pressure. Also, in this investigation, learners' involvement was used as a developed system for meaningful activity for the positive learning development of the learners (Ren & Zhu, 2023). Conclusively, this exploration connects with the study by Dai et al. (2022), who performed an investigation on the efficacy of ICT-supported teaching methods through the eyes of AT for looking at the satisfaction and interaction of engineering discipline learners and found that this theory is extremely significant for learners. This study also provides the identical conclusion given by Hajimaghsoodi and Maftoon (2020) in their research, which explored the students' achievement in second language writing while using computer technology. They also shared that the use of AT for learning develops a purposeful interaction between a subject and the object.

## Conclusion

The incorporation of smartboards in foreign language classrooms has been perceived as an innovative and powerful tool for supporting language acquisition. Smartboards serve as a bridge, allowing learners to utilise computer features seamlessly while maintaining communication. Furthermore, they have the potential to introduce new learning processes. Research indicates that smartboards positively impact student engagement, motivation, learning styles and comprehension levels. Previous studies have also suggested the benefits of using smartboards in EFL classrooms. Therefore, it is recommended to integrate smartboards into the EFL curriculum with careful adaptation of materials and systematic training on their usage in language classrooms. It is conclusively stated that the use of smartboards in local settings can not only enhance the confidence of learners and provide them with better learning methods but also boost their academic scores. Also, it would be a great advantage for the teachers. Smartboards are an integral element of technology-driven classrooms; rather, they are a mandatory aspect of every class. So, utilising them for English language learning in Pakistan can prove to be significantly magnificent.

## Recommendations of the Study

- Educators should undergo training to effectively integrate technology like smartboards into their teaching methods.
- Teachers need a clear understanding of the differences between traditional classrooms and those equipped with smartboards.
- Collaboration among teachers from different subjects is essential for professional development through sharing ideas, resources and experiences when using smartboards.
- Offering specific training programmes can help teachers effectively utilise smartboards in their classrooms.
- Internet and electricity smooth availability should be there in the institutions for the seamless running of smartboards.
- Future research should focus on further action research and studies regarding the educational integration of smartboards.

# 9

# MOBILE-ENHANCED LANGUAGE LEARNING AROUND THE GLOBE

Communication has been the cornerstone of human existence since ancient times, facilitating the sharing of ideas, emotions and knowledge among human beings. From early forms of communication to complex languages, our ability to communicate has played a crucial role in our development and societal progress. It serves as a bridge that connects individuals, fosters relationships and drives societal advancement. Without effective communication, society would struggle to function and evolve. With the changing paradigms in various genres, life is now unimaginable without technology. Earlier, people used to search for some wilderness where they could sit alone and enjoy personal time. In the existence of any language, communication is the most pivotal aspect (Ali et al., 2022).

The history of mobile phones is a captivating journey that began in the mid-20th century. The inaugural mobile phone call occurred on April 3, 1973, initiated by Martin Cooper, a Motorola engineer, using a prototype device weighing over two pounds. In subsequent years, mobile phones became more accessible, albeit bulky and expensive initially (Hossain et al., 2022).

The introduction of the Motorola DynaTAC 8000X in 1983 marked a significant milestone as the first commercially available mobile phone, despite its large size and limited battery life (Depot, 2009). The 1990s witnessed the emergence of smaller and more affordable mobile phones like the Nokia 1011 and Motorola MicroTAC, alongside advancements in digital networks such as GSM, enhancing call quality and coverage.

The early 2000s saw the advent of feature phones, integrating calling, texting and basic multimedia functions. Nokia's models,

DOI: 10.1201/9781003450733-9

like the Nokia 3310, were particularly popular during this era (Raghunandan, 2022). The game-changing moment arrived in 2007 with Apple's introduction of the iPhone, featuring a touch-screen interface and setting the stage for modern smartphones. Android devices soon followed, offering consumers diverse options (Holtzman & Goodman, 2012).

Since then, mobile phones have evolved significantly, becoming indispensable tools for communication, entertainment, produc-tivity, and more. They have revolutionised various industries and transformed societal interactions, enabling connectivity and access to information on a global scale (Raychaudhuri & Gerla, 2011). In contemporary times, smartphones have become a fundamental element in daily life, influencing how we connect, interconnect, work and engage with the world. They boast advanced features like high-quality cameras, immersive displays and high-speed internet connectivity (Banafaa et al., 2023). Mobile phones have redefined communication through instant messaging, social media and video calling apps, fostering connectivity irrespective of geographi-cal boundaries. Huwari et al. (2023) shared that mobile phones serve as versatile instruments for productivity and leisure, facili-tating tasks like scheduling, remote work and access to a plethora of applications for diverse purposes. However, their widespread usage has also raised concerns regarding digital addiction, privacy and cybersecurity, underscoring the importance of maintaining a balanced approach. Mobile phones also represent a convergence of technology, connectivity and convenience in modern society, shap-ing individual lifestyles and societal dynamics in profound ways. Now, mobile devices have become partners in their personal lives. In other words, most time is consumed with mobile phones rather than social-human interaction. Due to this, new words and terms are neologised. Now, e-relations, social media apps, selfies, e-con-tacts, fake reality, Facebook relations and X friends are common terms (Oktoma et al., 2023). One can hardly find anyone without technology. Rather, it has become indispensable in our lives. The apps and software that have gathered the world in the palm of an individual are indeed a magical revolution of technology. Due to this, mobile devices are popular among all ages.

If we look at every area like medicine, engineering, agriculture, transportation and so on, technology dominates them. Also, it has become valuable in education and academia. It has determined new ways for learning and teaching. The classrooms globally had some common characteristics, like

- Place-restricted
- Context-restricted
- Teacher-controlled
- Time-bound
- Dependent-learners
- Whiteboards, markers and blackboards with chalk (Klimova, 2018).

Gradually, there was the incorporation of technology into academia. The first wave was the infusion of computers into education (CALL). This was appreciated by the educational world, and this intervention of technology became beneficial for learning and teaching. The plentiful benefits of CALL were reported by various researchers. But obviously, the only constant thing with technology is that it keeps changing with time. So, almost 20 years ago, this concept aroused interest and was integrated into learning. Now, smart devices, tabs and other technological devices are more influential and common.

The process of language learning with a mobile device is called mobile-enhanced language learning. At the start-up stage, MELL devices were confined to IPODs, MP3, MP4 and other devices. Even these devices were welcomed, and learners and teachers appreciated them. Later, the introduction of Android and iOS mobile devices revolutionised the world of pedagogy. Therefore, MELL now enjoys popularity and acceptance globally (Gallagher & Savage, 2023).

Various scholars have explored numerous distinctive features of MELL with conventional pedagogics, like:

- Unconventional learning
- MELL is not geographically restricted.
- Time-flexible
- Independent-learning
- Learner-focused
- Universal (Hu et al., 2023)

Lately, the world is going towards apps to effectively meet their objectives in the world of academia. Now, classroom standards have changed, and this change is continuous. Almost all of the developed countries are using MELL and are benefiting from it (Reddy et al., 2023). Moreover, they are also coming up with new tech methods to increase interest amongst instructors and students.

Moreover, the use of songs and digital storytelling is also an additive advantage. Further, learners can learn through animated videos through MELL. At this time, the procedures, styles and techniques of imparting and receiving knowledge in an academic environment have completely transfigured. Access to learning through learning systems without geographical and time limitations has enhanced the effectiveness of MELL.

Now, the major MELL tool is mobile phones. Android and iOS phones are working like computers, with faster processors and large storage capacities.

Some key benefits of mobile phones for MELL are:

- Portable in nature
- Ease of usage
- Cost-friendly
- Smarter in design
- Easy user-interface
- Lower in cost
- Text, image and voice support

Going on, some other benefits of MELL are that it increases inter-student communication, listening, and speaking skills as well. It supports smart strategies of learning that can be influential in the acquisition of language. MELL classrooms are free from teacher-controlled learning. Thus, it gives the students the freedom to learn. Also, the teacher has passive contributions inside the classroom and even outside (Nikolopoulou et al., 2023).

With all these benefits and features, MELL is a valuable feature in various nations. If we look at American and European societies, we can see from the research that it has been more than 20 years since these societies have been using MELL in their academic affairs (Sinaga et al., 2023). Rather, in the early days, iPads and MP3 sticks were used for teaching English. Later, it was changed to mobile phones (Alam & Mohanty, 2023).

## MELL Integration into Education

Now let us look at MELL on various continents in academia. America has grown significantly in recent years due to the widespread availability and adoption of mobile technology among learners of all ages. The usage of smartphones, tablets, and other portable gadgets is common everywhere, and it is the same in academia. It has transformed language learning experiences by providing learners with an easy approach to the resources used in their learning endeavors. It has also provided them with opportunities for interactive practice, and personalised learning experiences. It has also provided a chance for teachers to inculcate the latest methods of teaching (Romero-Hall, 2021).

Though the United States is a native English-speaking continent, it is sensitised to the problems related to the conventionality of academia. So, it has moved to the use of mobile apps, online platforms and digital resources, which offer a wealth of opportunities for language practice, vocabulary acquisition, grammar exercises, and cultural immersion, and they all serve as MELL tools and paths. These tools cater to diverse learning styles and preferences, allowing learners to access content anytime, anywhere, and also providing mental comfort in learning (Alanya Beltran & Panduro Ramírez, 2021)

America is sensitised to the use of the latest technology and educational institutions across the continents, and it has embraced MELL as a complement to traditional classroom instruction. Teachers integrate mobile technology into their lesson plans to enable blended learning environments where students can participate in both face-to-face interactions and digital learning activities, and this has fostered learning prolifically (Kang & Shin, 2024).

Furthermore, MELL inventiveness in America accentuates the importance of leveraging authentic materials and real-world contexts to enhance language acquisition. Mobile devices enable learners to access authentic audio and video resources, such as podcasts, YouTube videos, news articles and social media content, allowing them to immerse themselves in the target language and culture.

In addition to formal educational settings, MELL is also popular among self-directed learners and language enthusiasts in America. Language learners of all ages and proficiency levels use mobile apps and online resources to supplement their studies, practice language skills on the go, and connect with global communities of learners and speakers. It can be said that MELL has gained value and has emerged as a pivotal partner for academia.

Looking at the Australian context, MELL in Australia has gained momentum in recent years, driven by the widespread adoption of mobile technology and a growing recognition of its potential to enhance language education. Australian educational institutions, from primary schools to universities, are increasingly incorporating mobile devices into language learning curricula to make sure they are up-to-date with the latest challenges in pedagogy and andragogy (Ahmad, 2019). The inclusion of the latest software and tools as digital resources for classroom education has provided the latest practice techniques for the engagement of students in cooperative learning situations. Australia has been proactive in promoting digital literacy and technology integration in education. Government initiatives and educational policies stress the importance of arming students with digital skills to thrive in a technologically driven world. MELL aligns with these initiatives by leveraging mobile devices as tools for language learning and digital communication (Ahmad et al., 2019). Australia's multicultural society and diverse population make language learning a priority. MELL offers opportunities for learners to engage with a wide range of languages, including Indigenous languages, community languages and languages of migration (Hebbani et al., 2023). Mobile apps and online resources cater to this linguistic diversity by providing content in multiple languages. Mobile apps offer interactive exercises, vocabulary drills, grammar tutorials and cultural immersion activities that complement traditional classroom instruction (Thai, 2015). Universities and research institutions collaborate on projects exploring the effectiveness of mobile technology for language learning, designing mobile apps for specific languages and proficiency levels, and investigating best practices for integrating MELL into language education.

Looking at the value of MELL in Africa, it has been gaining popularity in recent years, like in other parts of the world. MELL is driven by the increasing availability and affordability of mobile devices across the continent (Zelezny-Green, 2011). It is said that Africa has experienced a rapid expansion of mobile phone usage, with many people accessing the internet primarily through mobile devices. This widespread adoption of mobile technology provides an opportunity to use these devices for language learning. The African culture has become hybrid, so the languages are very varied, and even the dialects are also varied (Uwizeyimana, 2018).

MELL in Africa helps with language learning resources in ESL settings. MELL is also a low-cost solution, as Android and iOS phones are common. Therefore, apps, web platforms, and e-boards can be a good MELL tool and an alternative to already-used ways of teaching and learning (Viberg et al., 2023). It will also support collaboration and engage non-natives in ESL language activities. The use of social media forums and virtual classes will also enhance their learning. In many African countries, formal education systems face challenges such as limited resources, congested classrooms, and a deficiency of competent instructors. MELL offers an alternative or complementary approach to language learning by providing resources and support outside of formal education settings. Learners can access language learning materials on their own schedule, allowing for flexible and self-directed learning.

In a nutshell, MALL holds great promise for language education in Africa, offering opportunities to address linguistic diversity, overcome barriers to access and empower learners to achieve their language learning goals.

Looking at Europe, MELL has seen widespread adoption and integration into language education systems across the continent. Europe has been at the forefront of incorporating technology into education and using mobile phones for the purpose of language learning. It has aligned itself with this trend already. Many European countries have policies and initiatives supporting the integration of technology, including mobile devices, into education (Figueiredo, 2023). This support comes from both national governments and regional bodies like the European Union. Policies often emphasise the importance of digital literacy and the integration of technology across curricula, including language learning (Maliphol, 2023). Europe is linguistically diverse, with many countries having multiple official languages. European institutions collaborate on MELL projects, sharing resources, best practices and research findings. These collaborations promote innovation and the development of effective

MALL strategies. Projects may involve universities, language schools, government agencies and technology companies working together to advance language education. There is a wide range of mobile apps and platforms designed specifically for language learning in Europe (Torsani, 2023). These include language learning apps like Duolingo, Babbel and Rosetta Stone, as well as platforms for language exchange and virtual classrooms. Many of these apps offer gamified learning experiences and adaptive algorithms to personalise learning.

So, all around the globe, people are using MELL for varied purposes. It has also enabled the learners to construct their own frameworks for learning (Figueiredo, 2023). This will gradually replace the conventional system of teaching and learning, which will ultimately empower the learners. Also, the teachers have to change their roles. Conclusively, MELL induction into developed societies has created a new wave of fresh steps for the development of knowledge.

In an Asian context, looking at Japan, Singapore and China, MELL is cementing its place in pedagogy and academia. All these countries are using MELL in their education rigorously. Scholars have conducted various practical research on various aspects of MELL to examine and enhance its utility for teachers and learners (Nordin et al., 2017; Okumuş Dağdeler, 2023; Zhang et al., 2021; Zhen & Hashim, 2022). These countries have equipped themselves with the modern trends of MELL for ESL/EFL learning. But surprisingly, other South Asian countries like India, Pakistan, Bangladesh and Sri Lanka have not been using MELL. There are some examples and research on MELL in education, yet no proper structure has been devised to include MELL. Hence, their ESL learning is facing trouble and problems, and this is hurting these countries badly (Ali, 42024).

# 10

# MELL IN SOUTH ASIAN CLASSROOMS

Asia, being the largest continent globally, is renowned for its vast array of cultures, traditions and languages stemming from its diverse population. Education is highly valued throughout the region, with numerous countries prioritising the teaching of both their native tongue and English. The prominence of English can be traced back to historical events like British colonialism, which played a pivotal role in its widespread acceptance. Moreover, English frequently holds official status in many Asian nations and is a compulsory subject in school curricula.

Like the other continents, despite the cultural and linguistic diversity of Asia, education policies often prioritise the English language. This linguistic landscape underscores the importance of language in education across the continent. Additionally, there exists a socio-economic divide between privileged and underprivileged areas, with both facing challenges in terms of educational infrastructure and access to technology (Ali et al., 2022; Naz et al., 2022).

In many privileged areas, schools have better buildings and infrastructure, yet technology remains underutilised in classrooms. This space is also evident even in universities and higher education colleges. While multimedia classrooms and computer labs exist, the addition of technology, like smartboards, Palmtops and tablets, to educational practices is limited; rather, it hardly exists (Akkara et al., 2021). There is a need for greater emphasis on incorporating technology into education across all levels to enhance learning outcomes and provide students with modern learning tools and resources. The value of English in Asia is unmatched, yet the challenges of learning the language are increasing over time, particularly in terms of comprehension, syllabus relevance, acquisition of basic skills and confidence. MELL has gained traction in Asia due to the region's rapid technological

DOI: 10.1201/9781003450733-10

advancements and strong educational emphasis. So, mobile-assisted language learning (MALL) offers innovative solutions to the challenges of language learning in Asia, providing access to high-quality resources and support for learners. As mobile technology continues to evolve, MALL initiatives are expected to play a vigorous part in language education, both during and beyond the COVID-19 pandemic (Ali, 2022).

Overall, MALL holds great promise for language education in South Asian classrooms, offering innovative solutions to the challenges of language learning and providing students with access to high-quality language learning resources and support. As mobile technology continues to evolve, MALL initiatives are expected to have an increasingly central role in language instruction in the region.

The challenges facing language education in Southeast Asia can be effectively addressed through the acceptance of new technologies such as mobile-assisted language teaching (MALT). The COVID-19 pandemic significantly disrupted education services worldwide, resulting in learning setbacks. Many traditional classrooms transitioned to online platforms in response to the pandemic, with some education systems leveraging ICT and MALL applications to mitigate the impact of learning losses. The incorporation of computer and mobile technology into education will continue to have lasting effects on teaching practices even beyond the pandemic (Alghamdi, 2022; Ali, 2021). While access to technology remains a limitation for some districts and households, the lessons learnt from its application will be valuable as more classrooms and individuals embrace these technologies. The widespread availability of mobile phones and tablets, particularly since the advent of smartphone technology, has transformed learning by providing a multimedia platform for ICT-based interactions. Although investigation of the role of MALL on students' learning has yielded mixed results, the adoption of technology-based instructional tools appears inevitable. Technology is embraced primarily for its ability to enhance efficiency and offer new functionalities, contributing to increased utility. While prevailing studies have predominantly focused on the learning aspects of MALL, the potential benefits and implications of technology in education are undeniable.

# 11
# MELL Tools in English Language Classrooms

Mobile devices, especially smartphones and tablets equipped with internet access, have become an indispensable part of daily life for many people worldwide. This reliance is particularly notable among younger individuals, who extensively use these devices to maintain connections with friends and engage with the wider community.

Mobile-enhanced language learning (MELL) encompasses various built-in features and third-party applications that facilitate language acquisition. These include functionalities such as note-taking as well as audio and video recording capabilities, along with communication tools. While certain apps are specifically tailored for language learning, others can be adapted for educational purposes, thereby enhancing student involvement and fostering collaborative learning experiences. Though the many benefits of MELL are vivid, many language instructors and policymakers are hesitant to integrate mobile devices into syllabus design and classrooms. This reluctance often arises from a lack of familiarity with incorporating technology into teaching methods and concerns about potential distractions. Additionally, the wide range of options available on mobile devices can overwhelm teachers who are new to using them in instruction. Furthermore, integrating mobile devices may require teachers to adapt their traditional roles and instructional approaches, which can pose challenges.

Effective teacher training is critical to helping educators learn the best practices for integrating mobile technology into their pedagogy. Training of teachers is proportional to factors like school contexts, school policies on mobile device usage, student access to devices, internet availability and curriculum requirements.

 DOI: 10.1201/9781003450733-11

Despite these challenges, integrating mobile technology, such as smartphones and tablets, into language classrooms presents opportunities to enhance instruction through innovative methods.

Now let us talk about MELL tools inside the classrooms with reference to the basic skills of language. From many tools, smart mobile phones have proved to be the most effective classroom tools for English language teaching and learning (Kumar & Nanda, 2024). There are some default features, and some apps can be downloaded from the Play Store. Some already-installed features are

- Camera and editing
- Note-taking
- Video-audio and audio facilities
- SMS
- Internet

Whereas other third-party apps are so many in number. It covers everything from health to social communication, like

- Heart and pulse check app
- Weight checker
- Step counter
- Facebook
- X
- Skype
- WhatsApp

These apps were not precisely made for English language learning, but they have been used in various research studies to improve the English language skills of learners around the world. Moving ahead, there are purposefully developed apps that are tailored to specific contexts and skills. It is hard to write down the name of every app, so in general, one can say that there are

- Pronunciation development app
- English proficiency development app
- Flash cards for vocabulary
- "Contextto" app for vocabulary
- Grammar apps

- Reading improvement apps
- Quizez
- "Blackboard learn"
- Duolingo
- Babble
- Kahoot
- FluentU
- "Google translate"

# 12

## GAMIFICATION IN ENGLISH CLASSROOMS

### Introduction and Related Studies

In modern times, technology is enriched with technology, literally printing its value in all domains of life. Even now, one cannot separate technology from learning. The ambiance is technology-driven. The current learners can be called digital learners. One cannot separate technology from learning now. There are various instances and examples of technology and its utility for learning. There are various technology-supported strategies for producing effective results. If we look at English language learning or ESL learning, numerous ways have been adopted to overcome problems faced by learners in various countries and contexts. Some studies have explored the fact that already-established methods have been proven to be ineffective and have not produced desired outcomes (Dehghanzadeh et al., 2021). While some other researchers shared that motivation and confidence development are also important factors in uplifting the performance of learners. Consequently, various technological methods, like mobile-dependent learning, computer-dependent learning, etc., have been introduced to create positive outcomes. One of the latest developments in the ESL domain is gamification. Gamification refers to the use of games either purposefully developed or already developed for English language learning (Wulantari et al., 2023). This process has gained the attention of educators globally, and it is being adopted as a new way of teaching and learning. As the learners are strongly inclined towards technology, their strongest interest is in playing digital games, either on computers or mobile devices, during their free time. Initially started in 2002 and practically used by Bunchball Company for motivating its employees in 2005, this concept has gained huge popularity since the invasion of Android and iOS phones. According to an expert,

DOI: 10.1201/9781003450733-12

gamification is a learning innovation that includes games in a non-gaming ambiance (Zhang & Hasim, 2023). It was initially developed based on psychological aspects, and it is connected with the extrinsic and intrinsic motivation of the learners.

There are some major benefits of gamification, like:

- It engages learners effectively.
- It provides motivation.
- It develops confidence.
- It urges learners to participate.
- It creates a positive ambiance (Vathanalaoha, 2022).

In the context of second language learning, the pedagogy needs to always change. So, the teaching strategies need to be different to focus on the outcomes. A lot of investigations have expressed that L2 learners face a lot of issues and situations that are predicaments in their learning. To overcome these problems, gamification can be a good solution.

Some of the famous games around are as follows:

Duolingo is a gamification platform where users can move ahead at various levels. It is used on Android phones, iPads, iPhones, etc. It is focused on covering basic language skills along with grammar and vocabulary. There are six languages: English, Spanish, Portuguese, Italian, German and French, from which a user can select the desired one. The user can get an immediate response and it helps to track the performance easily. It is helpful for educators for daily usage. It encourages autonomous student activities focussing on collaboration and interactivity.

The next one is Class Dojo, which is used by the instructor to manage the behaviour of the student. It aids in motivating learners by applying various strategies that blend points, avatars and leader-boards. Parents can also get connected with the educator. It views, shares and assesses the learner's involvement with instant feedback. It lets L2 learners to adjust themselves to a new language by facilitating the process flexibly. It works on web, iOS and Android applications.

Another game is Edmodo, which is a social networking junction. It is beneficial to use for classroom extension at all stages of education. It is identical to Facebook, where participants can comment, post, submit their work and can check their progress. Moreover, quizzes can also be designed. It is also advantageous for open discussion ad posting assignments. it is a fantastic tool to elevate the motivation of the learner by teamwork and collaborative activities like the other games, and it also works on all the latest apps.

Apart from that, some other ones are:

Zondle: A gaming platform that is used for creating quizzes. It is perfect for practicing content and learners can be engaged without stress of learning. Socrative, which is used for various assessments through importing images and questions. It also shows live scores and instant feedback. It can easily be used on mobile phones. Finally, Brainscape, which is a flashcard-based game used for increasing the vocabulary knowledge of the L2 learners

Looking at the German literature, a study conducted by Basler and Dostal (2015) concluded that learners are spending 8 to 10 hours daily playing the games (online or offline), so already a harmony has been created that can be used for developing their language. Vathanalaoha (2022) pointed out that the learners' close connection with the game can be skilfully utilised for the specific development of language skills. In this way, conscious and unconscious learning can be possible.

Gao and Pan (2023) stated that extrinsic motivation develops a desire to participate and respond, and that comes from the content of learning, whereas intrinsic motivation is possible when interest is developed in something. As learners are inclined towards games, they are naturally motivated towards them. Nilubol and Sitthitikul (2023) stated that this motivation provides autonomy to control the learning process, develops understanding and collaboration, excitement and confidence, and finally enhances their creativity and performance. Adrefiza (2022) shared that gamification has become a significant factor in English learning as it constructs the problem-solving attitude amongst learners.

Another pivotal feature in this context is the design of the game (Yeşilçınar, 2023). Games are not components, but they are designed artistically and systematically to promote learning in a creative environment. That is why games have to be original and interesting according to the level of the current learners in order to attract them. Dehghanzadeh et al. (2021) reflected through their research that games are developed in a non-gaming context. The games used for English language learning have different objectives.

They are envisioned to develop general or specific skills in learners. Therefore, the strategy for using these games is significantly important. The proliferous utilisation of games without context and content can lead to the distraction of learners. Rahmani (2020) also supported the view that the application of games must align with the learning objectives; otherwise, it can prove to be useless. Therefore, a proper strategy must be developed to apply games. From this point on, the concept of purposefully developing games arose. Presently, there are several curriculum developers who are in line with the game developers to design such games that are germane to their learning needs. Tamayo et al. (2022) advocated this view that contextually designed games have proven to be more effective in meeting their objectives.

Some recent research shows that gamification creates interest among learners.

Dohny and Soekarno (2024) did a study on the incorporation of games into English language learning. Owing to the value of some games like Quizizz and Kahoot, they used the Quizwhizzer app as a tool of gamification in an educational context. The aim was to investigate the vocabulary development of 42 students who were in the pre-university stage. Using quasi-experimental research, their evaluation showed that the integration of games created a positive impact on the vocabulary development of the learners. It was also ascertained that Quizwhizzer improves learning like other language games and makes notable variations in learners vocabulary.

Argit et al. (2020) conducted a study where games were utilised for teaching vocabulary to fourth- and seventh-grade learners. The major tools for assessment were games, coursebooks and pre-and post-trial methods. The control group learnt from books, and the experiment group learnt from games. The final testing proved the difference in the performance of the experiment learners in contrast with the controlled group in terms of marks. This highlighted the importance of games in vocabulary learning.

Nguyen (2021) experimented while adding games to foreign language learning situations in a Middle Eastern school. He used a mixed-methods approach to extract results from 64 learners in grade seven. The preliminary scores were collected from the participants in the research for later comparison. After the intervention of a vocabulary game, the experiment group learnt through games, and the traditional learners used the previously used method. After that, the post-trial was executed, and data were collected for experimentation. The results documented that games proved to be effective in vocabulary learning, as the statistical performance of the experiment group was far better than that of the traditional group. This also stressed that games can be introduced for EFL learning.

All these pertinent studies reflect that gamification is an innovative way that has made its mark in various investigations. This also ascertained that adding up the latest ways can overhaul the previously used ways of using English in teaching and learning contexts.

However, in the indigenous context, there is a scarcity of research that has applied gamification to ESL and EFL learning. This investigation will strive to fill that gap by performing an exploration that looks at the importance of gamification in indigenous scenarios.

## Methods of Research

This research employed a quantitative research approach, focussing on descriptive methods to explore the phenomenon under investigation. Given the nature of the study, quantitative methodology was deemed suitable. The study's population consisted of individuals from Pakistan, specifically focusing on a sample from Baluchistan comprising 80 participants. These participants were selected from 7th-grade classes across five different schools, with 16 students chosen from each school. The selection of schools and participants followed a purposive sampling method, which was chosen for its effectiveness in providing cost-efficient and insightful solutions to the research problem.

## Stages of Research

The study involved learners who were attempting a 50-mark English B paper that consisted of different questions. One of them was an essay. Twenty marks were allocated to the essay based on a rubric devised by academic management. The research aimed to investigate whether games could aid in vocabulary development. To achieve this, participants were divided into two groups: control and experimental. A pre-trial method was initially employed, using a test as the instrument. Following this, learners were allocated to each group to ensure a mix of capabilities, mitigating potential bias. The control group, consisting of forty learners, utilised traditional learning methods, while the experimental group employed a vocabulary game called "Contextto" as a gamification tool. This process lasted for 20 days, after which a post-trial assessment was conducted, comparing the results of both trials. To ensure reliability and validity, variables such as age, gender, social background, class size, ambiance and medium of learning were kept consistent throughout the study.

Independent variable: games

Dependent variable: the learning of the participants

It is significant to mention it here.

## Results

Figure 12.1 presents data that has been visually interpreted through graphs. Upon examining the mean values in the initial tests, it's evident that the scores of both groups were nearly identical (8.57 for CNTRL and 8.58 for EXPT). Additionally, there is parity between both clusters in terms of standard deviation, as indicated by SN and T-values. This strongly suggests that both groups exhibited similar abilities prior to any intervention by the independent variable.

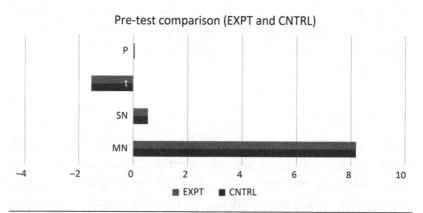

**Figure 12.1** Pre-test comparison of control and experiment group.

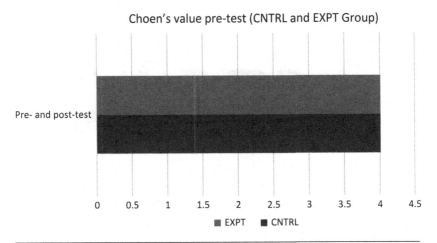

**Figure 12.2** Cohen's value of pre-test.

Figure 12.2 illustrates Cohen's value, which reflects the validity and reliability of the test. The difference in magnitude in the pre-test for both the experimental and control groups was measured at 4.01, indicating a medium effect size according to Cohen's d value (Cohen, 1988).

Figure 12.3 displays the values of both clusters following the experiment process, depicted using a bar chart. There is a notable difference in mean scores between the groups (9.18 for Control and 17.14 for Experiment), indicating a significant improvement in the scores of

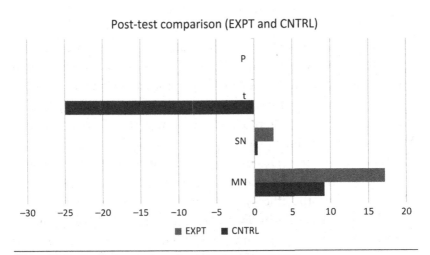

**Figure 12.3** Post-test comparison of control and experiment group.

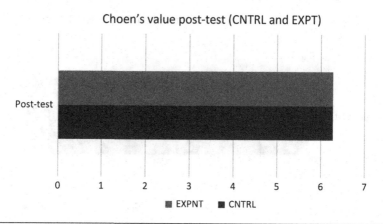

Choen's value post-test (CNTRL and EXPT)

**Figure 12.4** Cohen's D-value post-test.

learners in the experimental cluster after the intervention of the independent variable, almost doubling their scores. The standard deviation values were 0.43 for the control group and 2.53 for the experimental group. Overall, the post-test results confirm the effectiveness of the applied tool in the experiment.

Figure 12.4 depicts Cohen's value, which indicates the validity and reliability of the test. The difference in magnitude in the post-test assessments for both the experimental and control groups was determined to be 6.27, suggesting a moderate effect size according to Cohen's d value (Cohen, 1988).

## Findings

The statistical representation of the data has vividly portrayed the effectiveness of games on the performance of learners. The cluster that was studied by adopting the normal method (already used) does not have much variation in their pre-and post-trial scores. They had an 8.18 mean score in the pretrial and a 9.18 mean score in the post-trial. Whereas the experiment cluster got an 8.19 in their pre-trail and a 17.14 mean score in their post-trail. The scores of the paired sample t-test show a huge difference in the post-trial scores of both groups. Thus confirming the efficacy of the tool used for the experiment. It also shows that at the initial stage, both clusters' participants got almost the same score, but in the end, vivid variation is seen in their mean scores. Further, the Cronbach alpha value displays the tests' reliability and validity. Overall, the calculation of Cronbach alpha for pre- and post-trail authenticates that both trails are valid and reliable.

## Discussion

The study underscores the growing interest in utilising gamification for English language learning in grade seven, showcasing a promising trend in enhancing knowledge acquisition among future professionals. "Contextto," as a tool for gamification, has been applied for the demonstration of the potential for this method to thrive in academia. Various studies have shown the significance of gamification tools. Nilubol and Sitthitikul (2023) shared that gamification is the latest version that increases the interest of the learners. This is also seen in this investigation, where the learners developed an interest in vocabulary learning and gained new words. Consequently, their performance got much better in comparison to the control group.

In terms of motivation, the incorporation of game elements like points and rewards significantly boosts student engagement and intrinsic motivation, driving their language learning efforts (Gao & Pan, 2023). This characteristic of games can also be found in this investigation, where the learners demonstrated motivation, which increased persistence and willingness to undertake language learning challenges, leading to proficiency improvements across all language skills. Moreover, their motivation fostered their focused attention, helping them to develop efficient learning strategies and a sense of purpose that ultimately created a positive and enjoyable learning environment.

Adrefiza (2022) shared that gamification also enhances active learning and problem-solving attitudes by indulging students in interactive tasks and problem-solving scenarios, promoting collaboration and social interaction among peers. This feature was utilised here in this investigation; the learners were actively participating in their learning. Moreover, they were collaborating effectively. Further (Yeşilçınar, 2023) viewed that the design of the game is significant in that it gives immediate feedback mechanisms and progress tracking to further support effective language learning, which is a key component of gamification. This aspect can be found here in this research, in which the teachers tracked and monitored the learners' development and constantly gave them feedback. This helped them improve the performance of the students.

Tamayo et al. (2022) verdicted that games that are designed according to context create more impact than generally developed games. "Contextto" is a game that is designed according to the context of the language and follows the principles and regulations of the English language. This falls perfectly into the English-language context. Another angle in this regard has been shared by Rahmani (2020), who shared that the application of games must align with the learning objectives; otherwise, it can prove to be useless. "Contextto" is designed to have all the structural and componential resources that can improve the vocabulary of its users. Thus, in this research, the users, after using this app, learnt vocabulary better than the other group.

Going on, Dehghanzadeh et al. (2021) looked at a feature of gamification, which is the development of autonomy, critical thinking, and reflective learning. In this research, one can see that learners were autonomous, thinking critically and expressing the quality of learning positively. Overall, the research highlights the potential of gamification as a motivational tool in English language teaching, offering valuable insights for educators to optimise language learning outcomes in university settings.

This study aligns closely with previous research conducted by Dohny and Soekarno (2024), which investigated the integration of gaming elements into English language education. Their findings emphasised the significance of gamification in English language learning. Moreover, this research is congruent with Nguyen's (2021) study, which explored the effects of games on vocabulary acquisition among learners, advocating for the strategic use of gaming in English language education.

## Conclusion

This study proposes valuable insights into the amalgamation of gamification within English language learning. By examining the value of games and their impact on learner engagement in terms of vocabulary development. The results have demonstrated the potential of gamified methods to enhance the effectiveness of English learning experiences in an enjoyable atmosphere.

The findings emphasised the implications of using this method in a dynamic and interactive learning environment. Elements like digital-based challenges, interactive simulations and reward systems can elevate learners' moods and create captivating avenues for students. Furthermore, this research underlines the inevitability of continuing investigation and improvement of gamification methods, structure and use for English language education.

Conclusively, by embracing the benefits of games, curriculum designers, pertinent administration and teachers can all empower students for the cultivation of their language skills in an engaging and enjoyable manner.

### Implications of the Study

This research has implications for future researchers, as they can develop their own games to enhance the desired English language skills of their students. This study can be referenced for many other studies while connecting games to various genres of English. This study also had implications for the teachers to be encouraged to utilise methods to elevate learning. Further, in a country like Pakistan, this study can be used as an encouragement factor for the institutional heads to allow teachers to incorporate games into English teaching.

### Recommendations

From the eye of syllabi designers, the curriculum and syllabus should have activities that are game-based or encourage the use of games in language contexts. Moreover, the implementers – the campus managers should know the value of using games and must understand the concept to implement it rigorously. Further, the teachers should comprehend the effectiveness of using games, and they should feel confident in applying it as a technique to enhance their teaching. Also, on behalf of learners, they should be motivated to apply already-developed games that can be pertinent to their specific course for better learning.

# 13

# USING GOOGLE CLASSROOMS FOR DISTANT AREA LEARNERS

## Introduction

The new trend after the pandemic is to go for distance, online, or blended learning approaches, which offer numerous advantages compared to traditional classroom teaching methods. Among the most significant benefits are enhanced accessibility, flexibility in student scheduling and suitability for individuals with work commitments. Educators worldwide looked for alternative methods for tutoring and learning. This led to the widespread adoption and lasting popularity of Google Classrooms. Google Classrooms have emerged as a versatile tool for educators to manage assignments, engage with students, and monitor their progress effectively (Suparman et al., 2023). The platform's features address various challenges faced by educators and students in such environments, facilitating enhanced learning outcomes. Google Classroom, introduced in 2014, represents a blended learning approach that incorporates various functions aimed at streamlining communication in the classrooms, as well as simplifying the distribution and grading of assignments. The platform enables students to submit their work for assessment, thus providing them with an opportunity to receive feedback and grades (Sombria et al., 2023).

There are some key features of Google Classroom that include:

- the ability for instructors to create and distribute assignments as customizable templates,
- allowing students to personalise their submissions before assessment,
- Teachers can provide feedback and grade assignments digitally.

 DOI: 10.1201/9781003450733-13

- Streamlining the assessment process and ensuring timely feedback for students.
- Additionally, the platform enables the sharing of announcements, fostering communication and collaboration among students and teachers (Francom et al., 2021).

Google Classroom is believed to be advantageous for both students and faculty members owing to its range of features. For students, the platform offers communication channels and workflow management methods. It's paperless, so it naturally contributes to the development of efficient learning strategies. It also enables students to maintain organised files and reduce reliance on physical documents within a program (Umroh & Ismaya, 2024). The platform's user-friendly interface empowers students to utilise it effortlessly as needed. A critical responsibility for teachers lies in familiarising students with the application's functionalities, thereby enhancing their proficiency in its use. In Pakistan, where learning in conventional classrooms has become boring and uninteresting, learners are facing a lot of difficulty learning the modern trends in English language learning. Also, children's education is suffering due to the gap between societal learning and curriculum learning. Now, orthodox ways are no longer effective, and a strong need exists to induct ways that can enhance learning in a positive way. Particularly in remote mountainous regions that are characterised by severe weather, limited infrastructure, and sparse educational resources, the value of online education, chiefly by means of Google Classrooms, can be distinctive (Ali et al., 2022).

## Literature Review

Google Classroom, a service by Google, enables tutors and learners to engage in online learning activities. Viewing the evolution of Google Classroom reveals a progression marked by significant indicators since its inception in 2014 (Saidu & Al Mamun, 2022). Initially tailored for educational institutions, the platform required validation from school administrators for access by teachers and students. However, in 2015, Google expanded accessibility by introducing the Classroom API and a share button for websites, thereby facilitating engagement from school administrators and developers. Furthermore, integration with Google Calendar was introduced during this period (Putri & Adityo, 2024). The pivotal shift came in 2017 when Google removed the requirement for G Suite for Education, granting basic Google account holders the ability to host or join classes. This transition to public availability heralded a series of user interface enhancements, customisation options and expanded support for widgets and integrations, enriching the classroom experience. Notably, the year 2020 witnessed a surge in Google Classroom adoption owing to the global shift to remote learning prompted by the COVID-19 pandemic (Ali et al., 2020). In response, Google implemented various enhancements, including language support expansion, enhanced integration with learning management systems and the introduction of features like Smart Correct and Auto-Compose in Google Docs.

There are varied advantages to Google Classrooms shared by experts globally.

Omeh et al. (2023) said Google classroom platforms are the preferred choice for educators and administrators for improving teaching methods in an exquisite way. Google Classroom is welcomed for its user-friendly features that benefit both teachers and students (Gameil & Al-Abdullatif, 2023). With this platform, teachers can easily distribute assignments to all students simultaneously. One of its standout features is accessibility, allowing students to access course material anytime, anywhere, without installation fees (Pham & Nguyen, 2024). This accessibility fosters social interaction among students and a sense of belonging to their courses. Moreover, Google Classroom aligns with the theory of transactional distance, facilitating collaborative learning and interaction between students and teachers (Rahimi & Cheraghi, 2024). Moore emphasises the importance of conversation, structure and learner autonomy for effective learning.

Despite its advantages, Google Classroom has drawbacks for users. For instance, Google Calendar lacks advanced features, making managing due dates and materials challenging. Additionally, the absence of a notification tool requires students to manually update and stay informed about announcements. Furthermore, running an online classroom can be demanding due to the platform's requirements, including a stable internet connection and compatible devices.

**Writing Skills**

Writing holds a significant place in the domain of English language acquisition. It is classified as a productive skill among the four major language competencies. Writing is also widely acknowledged to pose challenges for learners. Unlike receptive skills such as listening and reading, writing involves the generation of language, particularly in the realm of English as a second or foreign language. Writing is an ongoing process driven by the author's conceptualisation of content and formulation of expression.

Furthermore, Gordyeyeva, A. (2023). defined writing as the creation of written language for the purpose of communication, emphasising its role as a means of conveying information. Nunan holds the view that writing is a highly complex cognitive task that demands mastery over various linguistic and cognitive factors. It transcends mere transcription, involving the mental activity of transforming ideas into written form, thereby serving as a lasting medium of communication (Basturkmen & Shackleford, 2015).

Despite its perceived complexity, teaching writing offers several advantages for learners, including reinforcement of language skills, development of linguistic proficiency, accommodation of diverse learning styles and cultivation of writing as a skill in itself (Paltridge & Starfield, 2016). It also simplifies the management of studies for teachers and facilitates the delivery of knowledge to students effectively and accurately.

When considering these perspectives collectively, writing emerges as a multifaceted process encompassing the endeavour to articulate and communicate ideas effectively to a designated audience, thus holding significant importance within the language learning domain.

**Google Classroom for Writing**

Google Classrooms has been proven to be promising factor for uplifting the ambiance of learning and teaching in an online environment. It is tailored to support collaborative, easily comprehendible user interface for the enhancement of students' writing motivation and skill development Wibowo (2023). The platform serves students to rally numerous features of writing ability, such as content, vocabulary, grammar, how to use language use and organisation. Numerous studies have shown that using Google Classroom leads to improved writing performance and a positive attitude towards writing. Blended learning approaches with Google Classroom have also resulted in superior writing skills compared to traditional methods. Additionally, Google Classroom meaningfully improves students' ability to acquire and learn English, particularly in basic language skills. In conclusion, Google Classroom adds value by playing a magnificent part in the development of the writing abilities of learners and also in elevating their motivation towards writing.

### Previous Studies on Google Classrooms.

A recent study by Nur'aini and Widiyanto (2023) investigated how Google Classroom affects students' motivation to learn. The study, which was conducted as a case study, had a quantitative research design. It involved 325 9th-grade learners. Using a random sampling method to select participants, the analyses were performed, and it was found that using Google Classroom positively influenced students' motivation to learn. Also, Google Classrooms increases interest in the procedures of learning, which engages students impeccably.

In another study conducted by Fadly et al. (2023), the impact of Google Classroom on students' writing abilities was investigated. Using a quasi-experimental research design, the researchers analysed data gathered through writing tests, where learners were tasked with writing on specific topics. A comparison of scores between two groups revealed that students in the experimental group, who utilised Google Classroom, demonstrated a positive effect on their writing skills compared to the control group, who followed traditional teaching methods.

Finally, in a study by Wibowo (2023), the perspectives of cadets regarding the use of Google Classroom for English writing instruction were examined. Using a qualitative research approach, data was collected through questionnaires and interviews. Descriptive analysis revealed that the cadets expressed positive views towards Google Classroom for their learning experience. Additionally, they indicated that Google Classroom could serve as an engaging and effective platform for learning.

Observing these studies, it can be concluded that Google Classroom has developed itself to be a platform that serves as a betterment for both learners and instructors. It also shows various advantages like motivation, collaboration and independence, which enhance learning. At the indigenous level, there is a shortage of research on Google Classroom. Therefore, this investigation could be one of the early ones and will help to lead others to conduct research from varied perspectives using Google Classroom.

### Research Methods

In this investigation, the descriptive method was adopted; the quantitative method was used. It is said that the quantitative method is a premier way to give perfect descriptive analysis (Ali et al., 2021). Participants in the research were chosen from Gilgit Baltistan. These participants were studying in government-sector schools in Gilgit Baltistan.

### Procedures for Research

The tool used for this research was an essay (test). These participants were placed into two groups of 100 each. This placement was not biased, yet all the participants were given an initial test, and on the basis of the score, they were placed into two similar skill groups. The contact hour for the experiment was 30 minutes, and later, the final test was conducted and the scores of both tests were compared by statistical analysis.

Some significant variables were found, like classroom settings, students backgrounds, English scores in previous classes, and the experience of the instructor. To validate this research, all these significant variables were made similar for both groups.

Also, the gender was only boys, who were taken to delimit the study.

### Result

Here, an independent sample (t) test was applied. This test autonomously presents the scores of each group, and it can be contrasted with the performance of the other group as well.

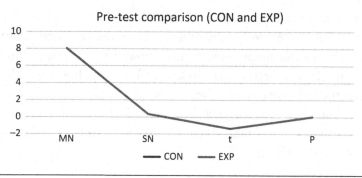

**Figure 13.1**   Pre-test comparison of control and experiment group.

This line graph (Figure 13.1) shows the values recorded for both the control and experiment groups at the initial testing stage. The value for control group's mean was 8.04 with standard deviation of 0.35 and t value of −1.35. In comparison, the experiment group learners were at the same performance level with the mean value of 8.03 and standard deviation of 0.35 and −1.35. Thus, there is no significant variation between the scores of both groups.

This line graph (Figure 13.2) shows the post-test stage scores of both groups. Here, we can see vivid variation in the performance of both groups. The control one mean score is 8.97, which is 0.93 better than their own score in pre-test. Whereas the experiment group score is showing a remarkable elevation with their mean score at 15.55, the difference is 7.52. This difference clearly validates the impact of the independent variable which was employed in this research.

Figure 13.3 illustrates Cohen's value, reflecting the test's validity and reliability. It was found that the difference in magnitude of the pre-test assessment for both the experimental and control groups was 6.09,

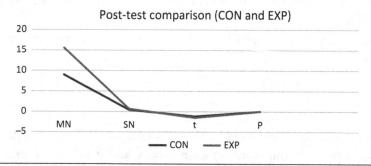

**Figure 13.2**   Post-test comparison of control and experiment group.

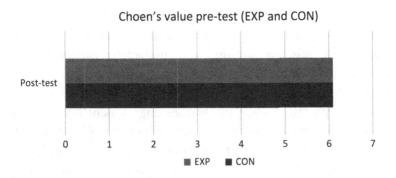

**Figure 13.3** Cohen's D-value (pre-test).

indicating a moderate effect size based on Cohen's d value (Cohen, 1988).

Figure 13.4 demonstrates Cohen's value, screening the test's validity and reliability. It was discovered that the difference in magnitude in the post-test assessment for both the experimental and control groups was 6.27, indicating a moderate effect size based on Cohen's d value (Cohen, 1988).

### Discussion

The findings reveal a notable performance inequality between participants in the experimental and control groups, indicating the rejection of the null hypothesis (Ho) and affirming Google Classroom's potential as a significant tool for English language education.

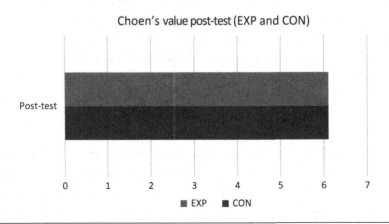

**Figure 13.4** Cohen's D-value (post-test).

These results resonate with Pham and Nguyen (2024), who emphasised Google Classroom's multifunctional role in facilitating task management, resource sharing, and interactive learning environments, thus accommodating diverse teaching needs and enhancing student engagement. Moreover, the investigation underscores the platform's efficacy in fostering learner engagement and participation, particularly evident among participants from Gilgit Baltistan, who found the platform's features conducive to a conducive learning atmosphere. Similarly, Timotheou et al., (2023) highlighted Google Classroom's capacity to personalise learning experiences and foster collaborative learning, ensuring no student feels excluded from the learning process.

Furthermore, the study underscores Google Classroom's versatility in offering a range of learning modalities, including online assignments, virtual discussions and live sessions, thereby affording learners flexibility and convenience in their learning journey. This observation aligns with Wibowo (2023).) affirmation that Google Classrooms have the ability to provide stress-free and adaptable learning environments. Additionally, Google Hangouts facilitates seamless interaction among learners, educators, and parents, enabling comprehensive monitoring of learner progress, a practice evident in the meticulous observation conducted by instructors in the present study.

Moreover, the accessibility and integration of various multimedia formats within Google Classroom, such as video and audio files, enhance the richness of learning materials, offering students diverse resources for assignments and assessments. Furthermore, the provision of voice comments serves to mitigate potential embarrassment for learners while providing personalised feedback, thereby fostering motivation and engagement. Furthermore, the emphasis on fostering learner autonomy is a significant element, and conclusively, this research lines up with Nur'aini and Widiyanto's (2023) investigation, which shows how Google Classroom affects students' motivation to learn and that by fostering a sense of mutual accountability and encouraging independent task performance, instructors instil confidence in learners to engage autonomously in their language development. These observations echo the findings of Haerazi (2023), who emphasise the influence of motivation on students' learning and writing proficiency. While various communication tools were utilised to facilitate interaction, students encountered challenges accessing internet data due to financial constraints or technical issues such as signal interruptions or power failures. In short, this investigation is identical to research performed by Fadly et al. (2023), who looked at the impact of Google Classroom on students' writing abilities and found out that Google Classrooms are perfect for elevating the writing skills of English language learners. In a nutshell, the findings revealed a marked improvement in students' performance compared to their mid-term marks, underscoring the effectiveness of Google Classroom as an educational tool. This outcome not only validates the utility of digital platforms in remote and underserved regions but also highlights the potential of targeted interventions to enhance grammar proficiency among young learners.

## Conclusion

In conclusion, the integration of Google Classroom as a teaching medium for writing recount texts demonstrates a significant impact on students' writing outcomes and facilitates communication between teachers and students. However, maximising its effectiveness may require additional time, effort, and innovative instructional strategies to enhance students' writing abilities. Especially in an area like Gilgit Baltistan where the learners have no organised classrooms, lack of infrastructure, intensity of weather, scarcity of furniture in the classrooms and lack of awareness regarding internet use. This study's outcomes are an encouragement to add up new digital tools for learning that can empower learners to not only learn better but also have access to modern and the latest learning material. This can also help them be aware of the latest trends in learning. Also, the instructors can have knowledge and awareness of modern learning problems and modern teaching methods, and they can employ the latest methods in their teaching, which can create a perfect learning ambiance. Adding up Google Classroom can serve as a network for creating a better education for local people. It can be shared that by leveraging digital platforms like Google Classroom, educators can effectively engage and empower students, ultimately fostering greater academic achievement and language proficiency.

# 14

# CHATGPT AND PAKISTAN

ChatGPT is an AI-powered chatbot that allows computer-mediated language to process like a natural language. It is used for communicating like humans. This is basically a language model for providing replies, creating emails and posts related to media and social media and writing content for the desired instructions. Also, it can go or provide videos and images.

It is somewhat identical to the customer service websites where an automated chat technique is used. ChatGPT is used for varied purposes.

This acronym GPT, "Generative Pre-trained Transformer", means that there is a specific instructional technological system that enables chat GPT for processing the resources and formulating the responses. It is developed to strengthen learning, incorporating human-like feedback for ranking the responses and improving the performance over a period of time.

If one traces down the history of ChatGPT, it is associated with OpenAI, which was research-based and who launched in November 2022.

The dataset used by it is huge, and it can easily:

- Provide answers to the questions
- Can generate responses for the queries asked
- Can be engaged in a human-like communication
- It can perform varied tasks

Just recently, GPT-4.O versions have been resealed and it is more productive, engaging and interactive as compared to the earlier versions.

## How It Works

To understand its working, one has to get knowledge of computer instructional language. However, in simple words it is operated by

DOI: 10.1201/9781003450733-14

the comprehension of text, also called prompts, for the generation of responses. It is a large model of language that functions as a computer-designed programme having the skills to understand and then produce natural language. The facility of deep learning helps the processing of data identical to the human mind. This permits to understand the language patterns in the form of words and then generating pertinent responses.

As the dataset is extensive, i.e., more than 45TB so, it has been trained to comprehend grammar, context, relationship and other significant functionalities. However, much work is still needed for its development.

### ChatGPT and Pakistan

In Pakistan, ChatGPT has gained instantaneous fame since its creation. In a country where the working genres are multifarious, its vitality has been accepted and appreciated by everyone across the board. Therefore, it can be a prominent and important tool that can be used for several domains, i.e., in education, it can enhance its quality by helping student to improve their Urdu and English language skills through practice, grammar correction and instant feedback. It can assist students in their homework for comprehension of some difficult topics and give them hints on preparations. It can also help prepare for the examination. It can assist and suggest ways for teachers, content creators and management to integrate inspiring learning ways.

In the local context, it can be a valuable resource for the customer services of any department where managing queries is difficult. So, using ChatGPT, several local language responses can be generated, and replies can be given with a cultural flavour to the customers. Also, by giving automated replies, it can answer some of the common issues of the customers, which will allow the human call centre agents to manage only complex problems. This can improve the overall efficacy of the system.

Then, it can be beneficial in the health departments (government and private) as it can provide generic information about common diseases, symptoms and their treatment. This can help to educate people, which can reduce anxiety and stress. It can also help to make an appointment for the patients. Importantly, it can also used in e-commerce where stores, sellers and franchises can use ChatGPT for their online services in recommending their products based on the references of the customers and history. It also permits to trace of the orders and can update the status of delivery. Furthermore, for any freelance activities, it can assist individuals in getting an idea to satisfy the needs of customers around the world. ChatGPT can also be used in governmental affairs; it can help to cascade information procedures and government policies like general information to the public, form and document filling in E-government services and also sharing valuable information and help on government portals. Pakistan is a country where English has a high value, so blogging, catchy lines and phrases, post-drafting and other attractive content in English can be generated from ChatGPT. It is also helpful in doing Urdu to English translation and sharing information with people.

Likewise, there is huge dissatisfaction in the local banking system with customer support, where businessmen have to wait for their issues to be sorted out. In this regard, ChatGPT can handle a balance check, a history of translation and information about a car or loan. It can also give financial guidance to the person who is in the process of making financial decisions regarding investments and savings.

Pakistan is a rural country where more than 70% of the country's is derived from agricultural affairs. ChatGPT can provide useful tips and information about local agriculture, which can be cascaded to the farmer. Moreover, some useful information on the cultivation and protection of the crops can also be easily shared with the farmers. Also, it can share weather forecasts and pest control practices.

In general, by involving ChatGPT in different sectors, Pakistan can improve its overall efficacy in various forms of life, which can overall improve the life quality for the citizens.

Conclusively, it is presented that being a new sensational technology, the future belongs to ChatGPT, and if used sagaciously, Pakistan can get maximum benefit out of it. Therefore, proper awareness, workshops and trainings should be given to people across the board in pertinent genres to better understand the use of ChatGPT in a better way. This can assist them in performing tasks in an effective and easier manner.

# 15
# WHERE TO GO FROM HERE

It seems there is a buffet of latest innovations in the technology restaurant. This linkage of information about technology creation, development and use is rapid amongst continents. If some app is developed in the USA, it is instantly known by people in Asia. In real sense, the world is now connected as a village. The inclusion of AI has added fuel to the fire. It can be predicted that in the coming years, AI will dominate society, and it will be the basic tool utilised for every software. In academia, currently, the world is stunned by the performance of generative AI; however, the AI assessment is around the corner, and assessment would be facilitated using AI-developed apps and software. Generative AI will create some problems of plagiarism, which will be managed by AI detective software, but importantly, the concept of AI and its usage should be properly explained to everyone; otherwise, there will also be of problems with students' learning and performance. In Pakistan, it can be predicted that gradually, the latest methods will replace the use of conventional ones and the blend of AI with modern tools can improve ways of learning. Also, for the teachers it can help to manage classrooms in a better way. Whatever the consequences may be, the next era will be the era of technology dipped in AI, and those who will learn will survive.

# References

Adrefiza, A. (2022). Using gamification in the English classroom: Impact on motivation and learning outcomes. *QALAMUNA: Jurnal Pendidikan, Sosial, Dan Agama, 14*(2), 537–548.

Afzal, A., & Rafiq, S. (2022). Impact of teachers' instructional techniques on student involvement in class: A case study. *UMT Education Review, 5*(2), 184–204.

Ahmad, K. S. (2019). *Integrating Mobile Assisted Language Learning (MALL) into a non-formal learning environment to support migrant women learners' vocabulary acquisition* [Doctoral dissertation, Murdoch University].

Ahmad, K. S., Armarego, J., & Sudweeks, F. (2019). Using technology to expand and enrich the vocabulary of low level English migrant women. *Immigration and Migration*, 43–98.

Ahmad, M., Shakir, A., & Siddique, A. R. (2019). Teacher-student interaction and management practices in Pakistani English language classrooms. *Journal of Language and Cultural Education, 7*(3), 115–134.

Akinnuwesi, B. A., Uzoka, F. M. E., Fashoto, S. G., Mbunge, E., Odumabo, A., Amusa, O. O., & Owolabi, O. (2022). A modified UTAUT model for the acceptance and use of digital technology for tackling COVID-19. *Sustainable Operations and Computers, 3*, 118–135.

Akkara, S., Mallampalli, M. S., & Anumula, V. S. S. (2021). Exposing rural Indian students to mobile assisted language learning: A case study. In M. E. Auer & T. Tsiatsos (Eds.), *Internet of Things, Infrastructures and Mobile Applications: Proceedings of the 13th IMCL Conference 13* (pp. 357–366). Springer International Publishing.

Akram, H., Yang, Y., Ahmad, N., & Aslam, S. (2020). Factors contributing low English language literacy in rural primary schools of Karachi, Pakistan. *International Journal of English Linguistics, 10*(6), 335–346.

Alam, A., & Mohanty, A. (2023, January). Learning on the Move: A Pedagogical Framework for State-of-the-Art Mobile Learning. In N. Sharma, A. Goje, A. Chakrabarti, & A. M. Bruckstein (Eds.), *International Conference on Data Management, Analytics & Innovation* (pp. 735–748). Springer Nature Singapore.

Alanya Beltran, J. E., & Panduro Ramírez, J. G. (2021). Mobile learning in business English its effect to south American students' learning styles in the covid 19 pandemic era: Its economic implications.

Alghamdi, N. (2022). EFL Teachers' perceptions on the implementation of mobile-assisted language learning in Saudi Arabia during COVID-19: Challenges and affordances. *Journal of Language Teaching and Research, 13*(1), 92–100.

Ali, M. M. (2022). The integration of mobile-assisted language learning: Perceptions of Pakistani pre-service ESL teachers. In C. Lorraine Webb & A. L. Lindner (Eds.), *Preparing pre-service teachers to integrate technology in k-12 classrooms: Standards and Best practices* (pp. 207–227). IGI Global.

Ali, M. M. (2023). Mobile-assisted language learning: A boon or a bane for Pakistani ESL learners?. In O. Sözüdoğru & B. Akkaya (Eds.), *Mobile and sensor-based technologies in higher education* (pp. 56–82). IGI Global.

Ali, O., Abdelbaki, W., Shrestha, A., Elbasi, E., Alryalat, M. A. A., & Dwivedi, Y. K. (2023). A systematic literature review of artificial intelligence in the healthcare sector: Benefits, challenges, methodologies, and functionalities. *Journal of Innovation & Knowledge, 8*(1), 100333.

Ali, A., Ali, S., & Parveen, I. (2023). Impact of using interactive smart boards on academic achievement of secondary school students. *Global Educational Studies Review, VIII,* 467–474.

Almetere, E. S., Kelana, B. W. Y., & Mansor, N. N. A. (2020). Using UTAUT model to determine factors affecting internet of things acceptance in public universities. *International Journal of Academic Research in Business and Social Sciences, 10*(2), 142–150.

Argit, G., Demirel, E. E., & Köksal, O. (2020). Teaching vocabulary through games: A comparative study of 4th and 7th grades. *Research on Education and Psychology, 4*(1), 41–53.

Asif, S., Afzal, I., & Bashir, R. (2020). An analysis of medium of instruction policies in the education system of Pakistan with specific reference to English medium education. *Sir Syed Journal of Education in Social Research, 3*(2), 370–382.

Attuquayefio, S., & Addo, H. (2014). Using the UTAUT model to analyze students' ICT adoption. *International Journal of Education and Development Using ICT, 10*(3), 75–86.

Azak, M., Şahin, K., Korkmaz, N., & Yıldız, S. (2022). YouTube as a source of information about COVID-19 for children: Content quality, reliability, and audience participation analysis. *Journal of Pediatric Nursing, 62*, e32–e38.

Bajunaied, K., Hussin, N., & Kamarudin, S. (2023). Behavioral intention to adopt FinTech services: An extension of unified theory of acceptance and use of technology. *Journal of Open Innovation: Technology, Market, and Complexity, 9*(1), 100010.

Banafaa, M., Shayea, I., Din, J., Azmi, M. H., Alashbi, A., Daradkeh, Y. I., & Alhammadi, A. (2023). 6G mobile communication technology: Requirements, targets, applications, challenges, advantages, and opportunities. *Alexandria Engineering Journal, 64*, 245–274.

Bangash, A. H., & Zahoor-ul-Haq, M. K. (2021). Factors affecting learning of English as second language in remote areas of Pakistan. *Pakistan Journal of Educational Research, 4*(4), 567–584.

Bastian, A., Liza, L. O., & Efastri, S. M. (2023). Revolutionizing education: How digital literacy is transforming inclusive classrooms in post-COVID 19. *Journal of Public Health, 45*(3), e609–e610.

Bazai, Z. U. R., Manan, S. A., & Pillai, S. (2023). Language policy and planning in the teaching of native languages in Pakistan. *Current Issues in Language Planning, 24*(3), 293–311.

Bhasin, A., & Lanka, S. (2022, February). E-learning-based collaborative learning experience in the education paradigm. In *Proceedings of Second International Conference on Sustainable Expert Systems: ICSES 2021* (pp. 1–10). Springer Nature Singapore.

Bhurgri, S. B., Sattar, A., Sultana, S., & Zehri, W. (2020). Problems in learning English language in rural areas of Sindh. Pakistan. *Journal of Education And Humanities Research (JEHR), University of Balochistan, Quetta, 10*(2), 82–90.

Bitrián, P., Buil, I., & Catalán, S. (2021). Enhancing user engagement: The role of gamification in mobile apps. *Journal of Business Research, 132*, 170–185.

Bitto Urbanova, L., Madarasova Geckova, A., Dankulincova Veselska, Z., & Reijneveld, S. A. (2023). Technology supports me: Perceptions of the benefits of digital technology in adolescents. *Frontiers in Psychology, 13*, 970395.

Budiana, K. M. (2021). The students' perception on the use of computer assisted language learning. *Journal of Applied Studies in Language, 5*(1), 174–186.

Butt, R., Siddiqui, H., Soomro, R. A., & Asad, M. M. (2020). Integration of industrial revolution 4.0 and IOTs in academia: A state-of-the-art review on the concept of education 4.0 in Pakistan. *Interactive Technology and Smart Education, 17*(4), 337–354.

Chaves, A. P., & Gerosa, M. A. (2021). How should my chatbot interact? A survey on social characteristics in human–chatbot interaction design. *International Journal of Human–Computer Interaction, 37*(8), 729–758.

Codó, E., & Riera-Gil, E. (2022). The value (s) of English as global linguistic capital: A dialogue between linguistic justice and sociolinguistic approaches. *International Journal of the Sociology of Language, 2022*(277), 95–119.

Cong-Lem, N. (2022). Vygotsky's, Leontiev's and Engeström's cultural-historical (activity) theories: Overview, clarifications and implications. *Integrative Psychological and Behavioral Science, 56*(4), 1091–1112.

Coronel, J. (2023). Practical technological tools for teaching and connecting with adolescent English learners in the post-pandemic age. *RELC Journal, 54*(2), 500–507.

Dahri, N. A., Vighio, M. S., Al-Rahmi, W. M., & Alismaiel, O. A. (2022). Usability evaluation of Mobile app for the sustainable professional development of teachers. *International Journal of Interactive Mobile Technologies, 16*(16), 4–30.

Dai, Z., Xiong, J., Zhao, L., & He, X. (2024). The effectiveness of ICT-enhanced teaching mode using activity theory on raising class interaction and satisfaction in an engineering course. *Interactive Learning Environments, 32*(1), 286–305.

Dehghanzadeh, H., Fardanesh, H., Hatami, J., Talaee, E., & Noroozi, O. (2021). Using gamification to support learning English as A second language: A systematic review. *Computer Assisted Language Learning, 34*(7), 934–957.

Depot, W. (2009). The evolution of cell phone design between 1983-2009. *Webdesigner Depot http://www.webdesignerdepot.com/2009/05/the-evolution-of-cell-phone-design-between-1983-2009/ [Consultado el 20 de Mayo de 2011].*

Dimitriadou, E., & Lanitis, A. (2023). A critical evaluation, challenges, and future perspectives of using artificial intelligence and emerging technologies in smart classrooms. *Smart Learning Environments, 10*(1), 12.

Dohny, Q., & Soekarno, M. (2024). Enhancing 21st-century learning: The impact of gamification with quizwhizzer on English language vocabulary acquisition. *Indonesian Journal of Educational Science and Technology, 3*(1), 45–60.

Engeström, Y (1987). *Learning by expanding: An activity-theoretical approach to developmental research,* Helsinki: Orienta-Konsultit, Online version Retrieved January 10, 2008 from http://lchc.ucsd.edu/MCA/Paper/Engestrom/expanding/toc.htm

Engeström, Y. (2001). Expansive learning at work: Toward an activity theoretical reconceptualization. *Journal of Education and Work, 14*(1), 133–156.

Eynel, O., & Koc, M. (2023). Turkish Classroom and Branch Teachers' Opinions about Smart Board Use in their Lessons. *On Humanities, Education, and Social Sciences,* 74–85.

Fadly, Y., Efrizah, D., Purwanto, D., & Aulia, Y. (2023). Enhance English language learning student based on Google Classroom. *Jurnal Scientia, 12*(03), 3822–3827.

Fan, H. (2023). Winter is coming? University teachers' and students' views on the value of learning English in China. *Review of Education, 11*(2), e3410.

Farooq, M., & Nauman, S. (2023). Teachers' perceptions and experiences of using digital technology in undergraduate classrooms in Pakistan. *Journal of Social Sciences and Media Studies, 7*(1), 54–62.

Fawaz, M. M. B. (2022). The effect of using smart board on primary stage Students' motivation to learn English. *Middle Eastern Journal of Research in Education and Social Sciences, 3*(1), 15–27.

Figueiredo, S. (2023). The effect of mobile-assisted learning in real language attainment: A systematic review. *Journal of Computer Assisted Learning, 39*(4), 1083–1102.

Figueiredo, S. (2023). The efficiency of tailored systems for language education: An app based on scientific evidence and for student-centered approach. *European Journal of Educational Research, 12*(2), 583–592.

Foot, K. A. (2001). Cultural-historical activity theory as practice theory: Illuminating the development of conflict-monitoring network. *Communication Theory, 11*(1), 56–83.

Frith, K. H. (2023). Using Technology to Facilitate Learning in the Classroom. *Teaching in Nursing-E-Book: Teaching in Nursing-E-Book,* 449.

Gabriel, F., Marrone, R., Van Sebille, Y., Kovanovic, V., & de Laat, M. (2022). Digital education strategies around the world: Practices and policies. *Irish Educational Studies, 41*(1), 85–106.

Gallagher, S. E., & Savage, T. (2023). Challenge-based learning in higher education: An exploratory literature review. *Teaching in Higher Education, 28*(6), 1135–1157.

Gao, Y., & Pan, L. (2023). Learning English vocabulary through playing games: The gamification design of vocabulary learning applications and learner evaluations. *The Language Learning Journal, 51*(4), 451–471.

Gogus, A. (2023). Adaptation of an activity theory framework for effective online learning experiences: Bringing cognitive presence, teaching presence, and social presence to online courses. *Online Learning, 27*(2), 265–287.

Gray, J. A., & DiLoreto, M. (2016). The effects of student engagement, student satisfaction, and perceived learning in online learning environments. *International Journal of Educational Leadership Preparation, 11*(1), n1.

Grigoryeva, L. L., & Zakirova, R. R. (2022). The role of English in intercultural communication: Past, modernity and future global perspectives. *TLC Journal, 6*(2), 45–55.

Hajar, A., & Manan, S. A. (2022). Emergency remote English language teaching and learning: Voices of primary school students and teachers in Kazakhstan. *Review of Education, 10*(2), e3358.

Hajimaghsoodi, A., & Maftoon, P. (2020). The effect of activity theory-based computer-assisted language learning on EFL Learners' writing achievement. *Language Teaching Research Quarterly*, *16*, 1–21.

Halai, A., & Durrani, N. (2021). School education system in Pakistan: Expansion, access, and equity. In P. M. Sarangapani & R. Pappu (Eds.), *Handbook of education systems in South Asia* (pp. 665–693). Springer Singapore.

Hashim, N. H., & Jones, M. L. (2007). Activity theory: A framework for qualitative analysis.

Hebbani, A., Mersiades, M., & Deshmukh, A. (2023). Exploring a mobile-based language learning intervention to improve English language acquisition and acculturation among migrants in Australia. *Australian Review of Applied Linguistics*, *46*(3), 395–423.

Herawati, S., Sundari, H., & Suciati, S. (2023). Teachers' experiences and perceptions in using interactive whiteboards in EFL classrooms. *Journal on Education*, *5*(4), 11592–11603.

Hockett, C. F., & Hockett, C. D. (1960). The origin of speech. *Scientific American*, *203*(3), 88–97.

Holtzman, J. M., & Goodman, D. J. (Eds.). (2012). *Wireless and mobile communications* (Vol. 277). Springer Science & Business Media.

Hossain, R., Hasan, R., & Sharmin, M. A. (2022). Short review on the history of Mobile phones. *Journal of Android, IOS Development and Testing Volume*, *7*, 33–39.

Hu, L., Hei, D., Wang, H., & Dai, X. (2023). Chinese College students collaborative Mobile-assisted language learning experience and flow as a key factor for further adoption. *Frontiers in Psychology*, *14*, 1165332.

Huseynova, S. (2023). Smart boards as a modern way of improving oral And Written communication skills In EFL classes. In *International Conference "Multilingualism, Internationalization, Digitalization As Factors Of Innovations In Teacher Education* (pp. 82–83).

Hussain, S., Shaheen, N., Ahmad, N., & Islam, S. U. (2019). Teachers' classroom assessment practices: Challenges and opportunities to classroom teachers in Pakistan. *Dialogue*, *14*(1), 88–97.

Hussein, H. A., Ahmed, A. M. H., Shawkat, S. A., & Kamil, R. A. (2022, November). The effect of using smart board technology on the educational process in the colleges of education in terms of features and challenges. In *AIP Conference Proceedings* (Vol. 2394, No. 1). AIP Publishing.

Huwari, I. F., Darawsheh, S. R., Al-Shaar, A. S., & Alshurideh, H. (2023). The effectiveness of Mobile phones applications in learning English vocabularies. In M. Alshurideh, B. H. Al Kurdi, R. Masa'deh, H. M. Alzoubi, & S. Salloum (Eds.), *The effect of information technology on business and marketing intelligence systems* (pp. 473–488). Springer International Publishing.

Jammeh, A. L., Karegeya, C., & Ladage, S. (2023). Application of technological pedagogical content knowledge in smart classrooms: Views and its effect on students' performance in chemistry. *Education and Information Technologies, 29*(8), 9189–9219.

Jang, K., & Landuyt, N. G. (2023). Limited benefits of technological advances in human service organizations: Going beyond the hype using sociotechnical knowledge management system. *Journal of Social Service Research, 49*(4), 426–446.

Jiang, L., & Yu, S. (2022). Appropriating automated feedback in L2 writing: Experiences of Chinese EFL student writers. *Computer Assisted Language Learning, 35*(7), 1329–1353.

Johns, A. M. (2012). The history of English for specific purposes research. *The handbook of English for specific purposes*, 5–30.

Jungjohann, J., & Gebhardt, M. (2023). Dimensions of classroom-based assessments in inclusive education: A teachers' questionnaire for instructional decision-making, educational assessments, identification of special educational needs, and progress monitoring. *International Journal of Special Education, 38*(1), 131–144.

Kang, H. S., & Shin, D. S. (2024). Mobile-assisted language learning during short-term study abroad. *Frontiers: The Interdisciplinary Journal of Study Abroad, 36*(1), 254–279.

Kaur, P., Kumar, H., & Kaushal, S. (2023). Technology-assisted language learning adaptive systems: A comprehensive review. *International Journal of Cognitive Computing in Engineering, 4*, 301–313.

Kearsley, G., & Shneiderman, B. (1998). Engagement theory: A framework for technology-based teaching and learning. *Educational Technology, 38*(5), 20–23.

Khan, J. (2023). An examination of newspapers' role in English language learning in Pakistan: Issues and recommendations. *Englisia: Journal of Language, Education, and Humanities, 11*(1), 199–208.

Khan, F., Fauzee, O., & Daud, Y. (2016). Teacher training, problems and the challenges: A comparative study between India and Pakistan. *Gomal University Journal of Research, 32*(1), 1–12.

Klimova, B. (2018). Mobile phones and/or smartphones and their apps for teaching English as a foreign language. *Education and Information Technologies, 23*, 1091–1099.

Kucuk, T. (2023). Technology integrated teaching and its positive and negative impacts on education. *International Journal of Social Sciences & Educational Studies, 10*(1), 46–55.

Kumar, V., & Nanda, P. (2024). Social media as a learning tool: A perspective on formal and informal learning. *International Journal of Educational Reform, 33*(2), 157–182.

Lee, K., Fanguy, M., Bligh, B., & Lu, X. S. (2022). Adoption of online teaching during the COVID-19 pandemic: A systematic analysis of changes in university teaching activity. *Educational Review, 74*(3), 460–483.

Leontiev, A. A. (2006). Sign and activity. *Journal of Russian & East European Psychology, 44*(3), 17–29.

Leontiev, A. N. (1978). *Activity, consciousness, and personality.* Prentice-Hall Englewood Cliffs.

Li, R. (2022). Effects of blended language learning on EFL learners' language performance: An activity theory approach. *Journal of Computer Assisted Learning, 38*(5), 1273–1285.

Li, K., Peterson, M., & Wang, Q. (2022). Out-of-school language learning through digital gaming: A case study from an activity theory perspective. *Computer Assisted Language Learning, 1*, 1–29.

Maidansky, A. D. (2021). Controversy and growth points in the activity theory in psychology. *Psychology in Russia, 14*(4), 3.

Maliphol, S. (2023). Mobile-assisted language teaching. *Journal of Southeast Asian Economies, 39*, S102–S119.

Marwan, A., & Sweeney, T. (2019). Using activity theory to analyse contradictions in English teachers' technology integration. *The Asia-Pacific Education Researcher, 28*, 115–125.

Masood, M., Asim, M., & Manzoor, S. (2021). Impact of technology on the behavior of students towards learning in Pakistan. *Psychology and Education, 58*(2), 9111–9113.

Ma, Y., Zhang, X., Abbey, C., Hu, D., Lee, O., Hung, W., & Rozelle, S. (2023). Computer assisted learning and academic performance in rural Taiwan. *Journal of Research on Educational Effectiveness, 1*, 1–24.

Meng, N., Lee, S. Y. C., Lai, W. Y. W., & Chu, S. K. W. (2023). Learning English as a foreign language through technology-mediated gamification in a rural setting. *International Journal of Smart Technology and Learning, 3*(3-4), 226–249.

Mujtaba Asad, M., Athar Ali, R., Churi, P., & Moreno-Guerrero, A. J. (2022). Impact of flipped classroom approach on students' learning in post-pandemic: A survey research on public sector schools. *Education Research International, 2022*.

Mun, S., Abdullah, A., Mokhtar, M., Ali, D., Jumaat, N., Ashari, Z., Samah, N. & Rahman, K. (2019). *Active learning using digital smart board to enhance primary school Students' learning*. International Association of Online Engineering. Retrieved February 12, 2024 from https://www.learntechlib.org/p/216524/.

Nardi, B. (1995). *Context and Consciousness: Activity Theory and Human-Computer Interaction*.

Nazari, M., & Karimpour, S. (2022). The role of emotion labor in English language teacher identity construction: An activity theory perspective. *System, 107*, 102811.

Naz, R., Nusrat, A., Tariq, S., Farooqi, R., & Ashraf, F. (2022). Mobile assisted vocabulary learning (M learning): A quantitative study targeting ESL Pakistani learners. *Webology, 19*(3), 1342–1364.

Nghia, T. L. H., & Vu, N. T. (2023). The emergence of English language education in non-English speaking Asian countries. In T. Le Huu Nghia & N. Tung Vu (Eds.), *English Language education for graduate employability in Vietnam* (pp. 25–48). Springer Nature Singapore.

Nguyen, N. V. (2021, December). Using word games to improve vocabulary retention in middle school EFL classes. In T. Le Huu Nghia, L. Thi Tran, M. Tuyet Ngo (Eds.), *Proceedings of the Asia CALL International Conference* (Vol. 621, pp. 97–108).

Nguyen, Q., Rienties, B., Toetenel, L., Ferguson, R., & Whitelock, D. (2017). Examining the designs of computer-based assessment and its impact on student engagement, satisfaction, and pass rates. *Computers in Human Behavior, 76,* 703–714.

Nikolopoulou, K., Saltas, V., & Tsiantos, V. (2023). Postgraduate students' perspectives on mobile technology benefits and learning possibilities: Insights from Greek students. *Trends in Higher Education, 2*(1), 140–151.

Nilubol, K., & Sitthitikul, P. (2023). Gamification: Trends and opportunities in language teaching and learning practices. *PASAA: Journal of Language Teaching and Learning in Thailand, 67,* 378–400.

Nordin, N. M., Embi, M. A., Norman, H., & Panah, E. (2017). A historical review of mobile learning research in Malaysia and its implications for Malaysia and the Asia-Pacific region. In *Mobile learning in higher education in the Asia-Pacific region: Harnessing trends and challenging orthodoxies,* (pp. 137–150).

Nur'aini, S., & Widiyanto, M. W. (2023, March). The effect of using Google Classroom as an English learning media on students' learning motivation: The case of students at SMP N 1 Juwana in the 2021/2022 academic year. In *Proceeding of English teaching, literature and linguistics (eternal) conference* (Vol. 3, No. 1, pp. 163–174).

O'Brien, H. L., & Toms, E. G. (2008). What is user engagement? A conceptual framework for defining user engagement with technology. *Journal of the American Society for Information Science and Technology, 59*(6), 938–955.

Ojo, O., Kareem, M. K., Odunuyi, S., & Ugwunna, C. (2022). An internet-of-things based real-time monitoring system for smart classroom. *Journal of the Nigerian Society of Physical Sciences, 2*(2), 297–309.

Oktoma, E., Nugroho, M. A. B., & Suryana, Y. (2023). E-learning as a platform in studying English among EFL learners: Benefits and barriers. *English Review: Journal of English Education, 11*(2), 405–412.

Okumuş Dağdeler, K. (2023). A systematic review of Mobile-assisted vocabulary learning research. *Smart Learning Environments, 10*(1), 19.

Park, M., & Son, J. B. (2022). Pre-service EFL teachers' readiness in computer-assisted language learning and teaching. *Asia Pacific Journal of Education, 42*(2), 320–334.

Peled, Y., & Perzon, S. (2022). Systemic model for technology integration in teaching. *Education and Information Technologies, 27*(2), 2661–2675.

Pervin, N., & Mokhtar, M. (2023). Reflections on doing narrative inquiry research: From the lens of interpretive paradigm. *Malaysian Journal of Qualitative Research*, *9*(1), 50–63.

Petchamé, J., Iriondo, I., Korres, O., & Paños-Castro, J. (2023). Digital transformation in higher education: A qualitative evaluative study of a hybrid virtual format using a smart classroom system. *Heliyon*, *9*(6), 1–15.

Poudel, T. (2022). Resisting the hegemony of English in Indian subcontinent. *Journal of Education*, *12*(1), 1–12.

Rafiee, M., & Abbasian-Naghneh, S. (2021). E-learning: Development of a model to assess the acceptance and readiness of technology among language learners. *Computer Assisted Language Learning*, *34*(5-6), 730–750.

Raghunandan, K. (2022). *Introduction to wireless communications and networks: A practical perspective*. Springer Nature.

Rahimi, M., & Allahyari, A. (2019). Effects of multimedia learning combined with strategy-based instruction on vocabulary learning and strategy use. *Sage Open*, *9*(2), 1–14.

Rahman, T. (2020). English in Pakistan: Past, present and future. *Functional variations in English: Theoretical considerations and practical challenges*, 127–148.

Rahmani, E. F. (2020). The benefits of gamification in the English learning context. *IJEE (Indonesian Journal of English Education)*, *7*(1), 32–47.

Rapp, A., Curti, L., & Boldi, A. (2021). The human side of human-chatbot interaction: A systematic literature review of ten years of research on text-based chatbots. *International Journal of Human-Computer Studies*, *151*, 102630.

Raychaudhuri, D., & Gerla, M. (Eds.). (2011). *Emerging wireless technologies and the future mobile internet*. Cambridge University Press.

Reddy, E. V., Reddy, P., Sharma, B., Reddy, K., & Khan, M. G. (2023). Readiness and perception of pacific students to mobile phones for higher education. *Technology, Knowledge and Learning*, *28*(3), 1113–1132.

Renaldo, N. (2022). Benefits and challenges of technology and information systems on performance. *Journal of Applied Business and Technology*, *3*(3), 302–305.

Ren, B., & Zhu, W. (2023). A Chinese EFL student's strategies in graduation thesis writing: An activity theory perspective. *Journal of English for Academic Purposes*, *61*, 101202.

Rizk, J., & Hillier, C. (2022). Digital technology and increasing engagement among students with disabilities: Interaction rituals and digital capital. *Computers and Education Open*, *3*, 100099.

Romero-Hall, E. (2021). Current initiatives, barriers, and opportunities for networked learning in Latin America. *Educational Technology Research and Development*, *69*(4), 2267–2283.

Roschelle, J. (1998). Activity theory: A foundation for designing learning technology?. *The Journal of the Learning Sciences*, *7*(2), 241–255.

Roshin, I., Shafi, S., & Masood, M. H. (2023). Enhancing ESL classroom management and language proficiency: A gamification approach in Pakistani universities. *GUMAN*, *6*(4), 221–234.

Ryan, J. M. (2023). Pandemic pedagogies: Teaching and learning during the COVID-19 pandemic. In M. Ryan (Ed.), *Pandemic pedagogies* (pp. 14–30). Routledge.

Sain, Z. H. (2023). Revitalizing education in Pakistan: Challenges and recommendations. *International Journal of Higher Education Management*, *9*(2).

Sandagsuren, D., Sukhbaatar, S., Navrasov, A., & Sultonov, Z. (2022). Lifelong language learning: Voices from the remote regions. In V. Kononova (Ed.), *Adult English language teaching: Transformation through lifelong learning* (pp. 83–99). Springer International Publishing.

Shahbaznezhad, H., Dolan, R., & Rashidirad, M. (2021). The role of social media content format and platform in users' engagement behavior. *Journal of Interactive Marketing*, *53*(1), 47–65.

Shernoff, D. J., Csikszentmihalyi, M., Shneider, B., & Shernoff, E. S. (2003). Student engagement in high school classrooms from the perspective of flow theory. *School Psychology Quarterly*, *18*(2), 158–176. https://doi.org/10.1521/scpq.18.2.158.21860

Sherwani, H. K. (1944). The political thought of sir Syed Ahmad Khan. *The Indian Journal of Political Science*, *5*(4), 306–328.

Sinaga, R. A., Febrianti, K. V., & Candra, D. (2023). The benefits and drawbacks of adopting mobile learning as perceived by junior high school teachers in Taiwan. *Interactive Learning Environments*, *31*(10), 6356–6365.

Singh, A. K., Rind, I. A., & Sabur, Z. (2021). Continuous professional development of school teachers: Experiences of Bangladesh, India, and Pakistan. In P. M. Sarangapani & R. Pappu (Eds.), *Handbook of education systems in South Asia* (pp. 1355–1380). Springer Singapore.

Siregar, R. S., & Sukmawarti, S. (2022). Development of smart board pakapin media in science learning class v elementary school. *Edumaspul: Jurnal Pendidikan*, *6*(2), 3034–3039.

Son, J. B. (2018). *Teacher development in technology-enhanced language teaching*. Springer International Publishing.

Srivastava, G., Nigam, N., & Kapoor, A. (2023). Transforming education: A significant leap from traditional to modern education space. *European Economic Letters (EEL)*, *13*(1), 71–77.

Stockwell, G., & Reinders, H. (2019). Technology, motivation and autonomy, and teacher psychology in language learning: Exploring the myths and possibilities. *Annual Review of Applied Linguistics*, *39*, 40–51.

Tamayo, M. R., Cajas, D., & Sotomayor, D. D. (2022, November). Using gamification to develop vocabulary and grammar among A1 level of English students: A quasi-experimental design. In *International conference on applied technologies* (pp. 177–190). Springer Nature Switzerland.

Tefo, R. M., & Goosen, L. (2024). Fostering pedagogical innovation through the effective smartboard instruction of physical sciences: Technologies in Gauteng schools, South Africa. In R. M. Tefo (Ed.), *Fostering pedagogical innovation through effective instructional design* (pp. 287–307). IGI Global.

Thai, B. (2015). Mobile-Assisted in Language Learning: From Learning Autonomy to Collaboration: A Case Study of Vietnamese Language Classes at The Australian National University.

The theoretical model of UTAUT suggests that the actual use of technology is ermined by behavioural intention. The perceived likelihood of adopting the technology is dependent on the direct effect of four key constructs, namely performance expectancy, effort expectancy, social influence, and facilitating conditions.

Tlili, A., Denden, M., Duan, A., Padilla-Zea, N., Huang, R., Sun, T., & Burgos, D. (2022). Game-based learning for learners with disabilities—What is next? A systematic literature review from the activity theory perspective. *Frontiers in Psychology*, *12*, 814691.

Tomlinson, C. A., & Imbeau, M. B. (2023). *Leading and managing a differentiated classroom*. ASCD.

Torsani, S. (2023). Teacher education in Mobile assisted language learning for adult migrants: A study of provincial centres for adult education in Italy. In D. Tafazoli & M. Picard (Eds.), *Handbook of CALL teacher education and professional development: Voices from under-represented contexts* (pp. 179–192). Springer Nature Singapore.

Tsai, M. C., Shen, P. D., Chen, W. Y., Hsu, L. C., & Tsai, C. W. (2020). Exploring the effects of web-mediated activity-based learning and meaningful learning on improving students' learning effects, learning engagement, and academic motivation. *Universal Access in the Information Society*, *19*, 783–798.

Ustun, A. B., Karaoglan-Yilmaz, F. G., & Yilmaz, R. (2023). Educational UTAUT-based virtual reality acceptance scale: A validity and reliability study. *Virtual Reality*, *27*(2), 1063–1076.

Uwizeyimana, V. (2018). *An investigation into the effect of mobile-assisted language learning on Rwandan university students' proficiency in English as a foreign language* (Doctoral dissertation, Stellenbosch: Stellenbosch University).

Vathanalaoha, K. (2022). Effects of gamification in English language learning: The implementation of winner English in secondary education in Thailand. *LEARN Journal: Language Education and Acquisition Research Network*, *15*(2), 830–857.

Viberg, O., Kukulska-Hulme, A., & Peeters, W. (2023). Affective support for self-regulation in Mobile-assisted language learning. *International Journal of Mobile and Blended Learning (IJMBL)*, *15*(2), 1–15.

Vitanova-Ringaceva, A., Kuzmanovska, D., Koceva, V., Ivanova, B., & Kirova, S. (2023). *Flipped classroom"–the future of modern teaching*. IATED Academy.

Vygotsky, L. S., & Luria, A. R. (1994). Tool and symbol in child development. In J. Valsiner, R. van der, & Veer (Eds.), *The Vygotsky reader* (pp. 99–175). Blackwell.

Wang, S. (2024). The dimensions and dynamism of group engagement in computer-mediated collaborative writing in EFL classes. *SAGE Open*, *14*(1), 1–18.

Wang, X., Hamat, A. B., & Shi, N. L. (2024). Designing a pedagogical framework for mobile-assisted language learning. *Heliyon*, *10*, 1–15.

Wartofsky, M. W. (1973). Perception, representation, and the forms of action: Towards an historical epistemology. In M. Wartofsky (Ed.), *Models: Representation and the scientific understanding* (pp. 188–210). Reidel.

Wibowo, R. A. (2023). The use of google classroom to teach writing at IVET university. *Marine Science and Technology Journal*, *3*(2), 58–67.

Wulantari, N. P., Rachman, A., Sari, M. N., Uktolseja, L. J., & Rofi'i, A. (2023). The role of gamification in English language teaching: A literature review. *Journal on Education*, *6*(1), 2847–2856.

Wu, W., Zhang, B., Li, S., & Liu, H. (2022). Exploring factors of the willingness to accept AI-assisted learning environments: An empirical investigation based on the UTAUT model And perceived risk theory. *Frontiers in Psychology*, *13*, 870777.

Yalman, M., & Basaran, B. (2021). Examining PRESERVICE teachers' use of SMARTBOARD and pc tablets in lessons. *Education and Information Technologies*, *26*(2), 1435–1453.

Yamagata-Lynch, L. C., & Yamagata-Lynch, L. C. (2010). Understanding cultural historical activity theory. *Activity systems analysis methods: Understanding complex learning environments*, 13–26.

Yang, Y., & Bao, W. (2023). Application of human-computer interaction technology in remote language learning platform. *International Journal of Human–Computer Interaction*, *1*, 1–11.

Yeşilçınar, S. (2023). Personalized learning through gamification: A ChatGPT approach to English language learning. In G. Kartal (Ed.), *Transforming the language teaching experience in the age of AI* (pp. 44–64). IGI Global.

Younas, A., SairaTaj, S. K., Hussain, S., Makhdum, F. N., & Khan, B. S. (2023). Classroom quality in terms of structural and process dimensions at early childhood education level in Pakistan. *Journal of Positive School Psychology*, *7*(1), 79–94.

Yucedal, H. M. (2023). Integration of web 2.0 tools in EFL classes: Barriers and solutions. *Revista Amazonia Investiga*, *12*(63), 109–122.

Zaman, K. U., & Anwar, T. (2023). Investigating science teachers' technology integration in classrooms. A case study of a private higher secondary school in Karachi, Pakistan. *Education and Information Technologies*, *1*, 1–20.

Zelezny-Green, R. (2011). The potential impact of mobile-assisted language learning on women and girls in Africa: A literature review. *Ubiquitous Learning*, *3*(1), 69.

Zhang, S., & Hasim, Z. (2023). Gamification in EFL/ESL instruction: A systematic review of empirical research. *Frontiers in Psychology*, *13*, 1030790.

Zhang, Y., Zhang, L., Chen, T., Lin, H., Ye, S., Du, J., & Chen, C. (2021, October). Acceptance and Use of Mobile-Assisted Language Learning for Vocational College Students. In *International Conference on 5G for Future Wireless Networks* (pp. 573–589). Springer International Publishing.

Zhang, R., Zou, D., & Cheng, G. (2024). Technology-enhanced language learning with null and negative results since 2000: A systematic review based on the activity theory. *Education and Information Technologies*, *29*(4), 5017–5077.

Zhen, L. S., & Hashim, H. (2022). The usage of mall in learners' readiness to speak English. *Sustainability*, *14*(23), 16227.

Žižek, S. (2018). *Like a thief in broad daylight: Power in the era of post-humanity*. Penguin UK.

Printed in the United States
by Baker & Taylor Publisher Services